Between Mountains

The Inevitable Return To The Valley

John Rivera

VIVE CONSULTING

Contents

Contents

Acknowledgments

This book is dedicated with heartfelt love to my Lord and Savior, Jesus Christ. His gentle whispers have touched my soul and filled every page of this book. His constant presence in my life has healed me time and again, gifting me with a profound sense of purpose and direction. I'm thrilled to share how my incredible experiences with Him have genuinely shaped my journey and deepened my relationship with Him. Without His loving guidance, I genuinely believe I would be lost, wandering through life without the deep meaning and fulfillment that comes from knowing Him closely.

I want to also take a moment to express gratitude to my amazing wife, Naomi, and our much-loved sons, Zachary and Matthew. Your steadfast love and daily inspirations have been my guiding lights, always encouraging me as I pursue my many dreams. I am so grateful for the unwavering support you provide —it truly fuels my passion and creativity. I love you all dearly and treasure every single moment we share together!

This book is also dedicated with sincere appreciation to the many leaders who inspire us each day. These exceptional individuals pour their hearts into their journeys, skillfully navigating the myriads of challenges that life presents. Their remarkable paths, often marked by stunning mountains and daunting valleys, reflect their struggles and victories as well as their unwavering commitment to their purpose, which ultimately paves the way for countless others to join them in this incredible journey of faith, growth, and discovery.

"God is not unjust; he will not forget your work and the love you have shown him as you have helped his people and continue to help them." (Hebrews 6:10)

Foreword

If you are like me, you might find it easier to understand certain concepts when they are presented step by step. I truly appreciate when authors encourage readers to explore all the different elements of a book, as this approach promotes a deeper understanding of the material and fosters active engagement with the content. This way, the key insights become more accessible and, hopefully, easier to apply in our daily lives.

If that's you, you will love this book by John Rivera. As I read through it, I discovered that each chapter addresses a crucial topic of effective leadership. I appreciated how his principles are presented for ministry, business, and non-profits. I especially admired how John gets straight to the nitty-gritty of applying these principles to succeed in each area of leadership. Furthermore, his real-world examples provide a practical context that enhances understanding and implementation. You will likely find yourself inspired and motivated to take actionable steps toward becoming better leaders in your respective fields.

If you find yourself among those folks who often struggle to uncover inspiring quotes from influential figures in both spiritual and secular realms, your search ends here. This book is brimming with remarkable quotes and vivid illustrations sourced from some of history's most esteemed orators and profound thinkers. Whether you seek wisdom for personal reflection or motivation in your business or ministry endeavors, this book provides a wealth of inspiration that can resonate with a diverse audience.

John's extensive experience in ministry and para-church organizations shines through in the leadership insights and applications presented throughout the book. He truly understands the challenges of leadership in today's world, as we often find ourselves "between mountains" of decisions while executing the necessary actions to make a difference as leaders. His unique perspective, shaped by years of navigating complex situations, provides practical strategies to overcome obstacles. Furthermore, his capacity to convey these ideas will encourage more profound reflection and development among aspiring leaders eager to initiate practical change.

I have had the honor of knowing John and his wonderful family for many years, and at one point, I served as his pastor in our local church. John continues to serve the local church with great success; he is also a voice, mentor, and coach to numerous ministries across the nation.

Get ready for a great adventure into leadership concepts and virtues at their finest as you delve into this book. While navigating your journey through life between mountains, make sure to savor the experience... I truly did!

Rev. Don James Superintendent,
New Jersey Ministry Network, Assemblies of God

Purpose of This Book

In the following chapters, I'm excited to share numerous strategies and essential principles that will help you navigate through those inevitable valley experiences—those challenging times in life that can often feel overwhelming. As you work your way through these pages, I hope you'll take a moment to reflect on how you can apply these ideas to your own valley experiences or prepare yourself for future hurdles. Think of these pages as your personal road map. Feel free to jot down your thoughts, plans, prayers, and insights. It's not just about reading; it's about learning and encouraging yourself to grow, so you can ultimately make a positive impact on others and fully embrace everything life has to offer.

As you explore these lessons, I want you to think of the valleys as a variety of challenges we might face along the way — like personal loss, financial difficulties, career setbacks, or times filled with doubt and confusion. Each valley may touch us in different ways, yet they often bring about similar feelings of uncertainty and pressure. Even if you're not in a valley right now, you're likely either about to enter one or working to rise up from a challenging time. Recognizing the signs of these valleys is the first step to meeting them with readiness and strength.

Understanding these experiences is incredibly important because they aren't merely obstacles to overcome; they are also amazing opportunities for growth and self-discovery. Every challenge we encounter offers us wonderful lessons about our minds and hearts. They also reveal how well we're equipped to respond to the needs of those around us. When we learn to navigate these valleys, we find insights that empower us to grow and evolve. It's important that we shift our perspective and see these tough times as chances for personal development rather than just tests to endure. By viewing our valley experiences this way, we can embrace them warmly as necessary steps on our voyage, leading us toward new understandings of what we genuinely cherish and seek in life.

As you walk through these valleys, you may uncover profound insights that reveal who you really are, along with the unique path you're meant to follow. This process of introspection often takes us deep within ourselves, helping us confront our inner thoughts and feelings. In doing so, we gain a better understanding of our strengths and weaknesses, as well as our dreams and fears. This kind of self-discovery is important, as it can ignite a renewed sense of purpose in our lives. The challenges we face shift from being obstacles to becoming transformative experiences that shape us and guide our journey toward authenticity.

Seeing the lessons in our life experiences can genuinely boost your personal growth and resilience. When we embrace the challenges that come our way, we lay down a stronger foundation to tackle whatever comes next. When we look at each hurdle as a chance to grow, it deepens our understanding and appreciation of our unique experience. As we learn to steer through these challenging times, we not only gain a clearer sense of who we are but also open our hearts to others who might be facing similar struggles. This enhanced awareness can fill our lives with so much more meaning and joy.

Are you ready to start an exciting journey towards lasting success and continuous growth? I believe you are! Together, we're about to take this transformative step towards personal growth and self-discovery. This journey isn't just about reaching goals; it's about growing as individuals and building resilience when faced with challenges. Each chapter you encounter will be a special moment in your story, encouraging you to step outside your comfort zone and tackle obstacles head-on. Embrace this wonderful chance to dive deep into your potential, and remember, every little step you take brings you closer to becoming the best version of yourself.

As you dive into these chapters, I invite you to keep your heart and mind open to welcome all the new lessons that await you. Embrace each experience with a willingness to learn as you trek through the ever-changing landscape of your life. Remember, staying humble is key—so be ready to accept the insights and guidance that will surely come your way. Some lessons may challenge you and make you feel a bit uneasy. However, they will lead to important decisions, so I encourage you to embrace these experiences and trust the process. This path is overflowing with opportunities to learn, and being open to gaining knowledge from every situation paves the way for genuine development. Have faith that the wisdom you gather, along with your determination and perseverance, will guide you to amazing outcomes, enriching your life and the lives of those around you!

The Valley And The Ascent

Leadership Beyond The Summit

Leadership is often celebrated during those exciting moments of achievement— when awards are received, goals are met, and leaders take a moment to relish their accomplishments. However, true leadership dives deeper than these highlights; it blossoms in the valleys of life, where challenges, setbacks, and tough times help to build resilience and character. It's in these lower moments that leaders are shaped, demonstrating their remarkable ability to inspire, uplift, and create positive change in the lives of individuals, organizations, and entire communities.

Even when I walk through the darkest valley, I will not be afraid, for you are close beside me. Your rod and your staff protect and comfort me.

— Psalm 23:4

The true nature of the "valley" struck me during a recent agonizing season in my life. As a matter of fact, this book is a byproduct of that experience and the lessons I learned during that time. As I navigated this "valley of shadows," my perception was transformed; what I had previously viewed as secure, safe, and friendly now felt unstable, unsafe, and hostile. As a result of this valley season, uncertainty became my new reality. At first, I felt anxious and started to doubt myself, questioning God along the way. I metaphorically dug a hole, wishing to make the issue disappear. I also prayed for a quick fix to eliminate the circumstances creating such pain. But, as life often reveals, that wasn't how it would unfold.

It took many months for a resolution to materialize. During that time, I felt moved to create a recovery and survival strategy based on biblical truth to make room for God's gentle guidance. After a season of struggle and seeking the Lord's direction, I began to see a glimmer of hope at the end of the tunnel, and my faith began to bloom once again. As I traversed through this thorny and problematic valley, I realized that not only were my circumstances changing, but I was also experiencing significant personal growth. The valley was reshaping me, and I began to embrace this transformation, allowing it to profoundly impact my life for a greater purpose.

During my time in this valley, I also discovered a deeper reliance on God's word – more than ever before. I embraced the comforting truth that "faith comes by hearing, and hearing by the word of God" (Romans 10:17). I wasn't searching for a miraculous or emotional experience, butterflies, or even an angel visiting my room; my heart desired to hear God's voice through His Word.

As I shared my longings with Him in prayer and meditation, He faithfully met me each morning through the Scriptures, bringing refreshing insight each time. This journey enriched my faith in ways that past decades hadn't achieved. I began to grasp God's heart in a profoundly personal way, training my eyes and ears to respond like a child to a loving Father. I stayed engaged in seeking resolutions to my valley season, but not in my own strength. I learned to wait on Him, relying on His guidance and wisdom. I felt assured that He was providing and leading me beyond what I could comprehend. This understanding filled me with peace and strength, empowering me to step into the unfamiliar territory of saying yes to Him "in advance" of the answer or miracle.

In 2020, Rev. Tim Keller faced his lowest point, compelling him to trust God more than ever. His battle with stage 4 pancreatic cancer illustrates how to endure challenging situations with unwavering faith. Confronted with a serious diagnosis, he fully entrusted his life to God, which enriched his prayer life and strengthened his belief. Rather than surrendering to fear, he sought the presence of God and found solace in the certainty of divine guidance over his life. Just as Keller navigated his turbulent path with God's support, we too can find resilience in our darkest hours by clinging to His promises. Isaiah 41:10 reminds us: "Fear not, for I am with you; be not dismayed, for I am your God; I will strengthen you, I will help you, I will uphold you with my righteous right hand." No valley is too deep when we depend on God, who sustains and guides us through each storm.

Leadership in the Valleys: A Biblical Perspective

Just like the changing seasons in our lives while in the valley, the Bible is replete with stories of leaders who encountered powerful lessons and made a lasting impact as a result of their own valley experiences. Take Joseph's story from Genesis, for example. After being betrayed by his brothers, sold into slavery, and unjustly imprisoned, he faced many tough times filled with challenges and uncertainty. However, it was during these diffi-cult moments that he built the character, wisdom, and resilience needed to eventually rise to the second-in-command after Pharaoh. In doing so, he saved Egypt from famine and showed profound compassion to his brothers, bringing his family back together (Genesis 50:20). Joseph's incredible journey reminds us that the challenges faced in the valley can truly prepare us for the great responsibilities that await us at the summit.

In a similar way, David's story beautifully illustrates how true leadership shines through adversity. Before he became the king of Israel, David faced many years on the run from King Saul, navigating feelings of isolation, experiencing betrayal, and carrying the heavy mantle of leadership as an outlaw. These challenging times in the "valley" shaped David into a leader who was after God's own heart, enabling him to unite a divided kingdom and guide his people with passion and integrity (1 Samuel 16-31; Psalm 23).

Jesus also demonstrated what true leadership looks like, reaching far beyond the peak moments. We read that, when He heard of John the Baptist's death, Jesus sought a moment of soli-tude to mourn, but the crowds followed Him, longing for His teaching. Despite His own sorrow, He responded with compas-sion, welcoming and ministering to them. This reflects the reality of ministry—leading with grace even in personal valleys, recognizing the needs of others, and serving with a heart of love. Authentic leadership is often marked by the ability to set aside personal pain to care for those who are hurting. Ultimately, Jesus' most profound acts of leadership weren't in the spotlight of miracles but in the quiet strength and humility he displayed while enduring the suffering of the cross. As Philippians 2:8 reminds us, "And being found in appearance as a man, he humbled himself by becoming obedient to death—even death on a cross!" Through selfless leadership in his lowest valleys, Jesus offered redemption that transformed the world, offering us the ultimate example of what it means to lead with a servant's heart.

Historical Leaders: Proving Grounds in the Valleys

History is filled with leaders whose journeys were deeply influenced by their experiences in the valleys of life. Take Abraham Lincoln, for example. His leadership during the American Civil War not only helped preserve the United States but also played a pivotal role in ending slavery. Before he reached the heights of his presidency, Lincoln faced a host of personal and professional challenges, including business failures, political defeats, and the heartbreaking loss of loved ones. Yet, these very struggles shaped his incredible empathy, resilience, and determination, allowing him to guide the nation through its darkest times. His iconic Gettysburg Address, a true testament to his spirit, continues to inspire generations to this day.

Winston Churchill's leadership during World War II exemplifies determination. Before becoming Prime Minister, he faced considerable challenges and criticism for his earlier decisions in World War I. However, it was during these trying times, these "valleys," that Churchill developed the strength and vision necessary to lead Britain through its most significant trials. Despite his struggle with what he called his "black dog," representing the depression and melancholy he often experienced, he is widely seen as a resilient and courageous leader. He managed to overcome this personal battle while steering Britain through a critical period in history, playing an essential role in World War II. His capacity to face his internal darkness while guiding the nation through significant challenges reflects his extraordinary strength and resolve. His memorable words, "Never give in," capture the spirit of resilience that emerged in the face of adversity, highlighting how these valleys prepare leaders for the heights ahead.

Leadership Lessons for Today's World

The valleys of leadership—moments of failure, loss, and adversity—are where character is tested, shaped, and strengthened. For those who wish to make a positive impact on lives, organizations, and societies, these experiences are incredibly valuable. They help leaders develop empathy, embrace change, and tackle challenges with courage and creativity.

In organizations, leaders often encounter these "valley moments" through challenges like financial crises, employee turnover, or resistance to change. Great leaders make the most of these times by building trust, fostering hope, and rallying their teams around common goals. A wonderful example is Howard Schultz, the former CEO of Starbucks, who displayed remarkable leadership when he returned to the company during a tough financial period. By reconnecting with Starbucks' core mission and values, Schultz revitalized the organization and showed that leadership is about steadfastness and a clear vision, even during hard times.

Leadership in the valley flourishes when grounded in humility and an honest eagerness to learn from our experiences. As Theodore Roosevelt wisely remarked, "It is not the critic who counts... The credit belongs to the man who is actually in the arena, whose face is marred by dust and sweat and blood." Embracing this mindset is essential for leaders who want to make a real difference. By cherishing the invaluable lessons learned in the valley, leaders nurture the resilience and authenticity that empower them to face challenges head-on and uplift those around them.

Tying It All Together: Transformational Leadership

One thing that ties together these examples—whether from the Bible, history, or today—is that true leadership isn't just about celebrating victories; it's also about finding the strength to bounce back from challenges with a renewed sense of purpose. It's during these tough times that leaders often discover their "why," learn to align their actions with their core values, and cultivate the empathy needed to truly connect with those they serve.

Scripture underscores this truth in James 1:2-4: "*Consider it pure joy, my brothers and sisters, whenever you face trials of many kinds, because you know that the testing of your faith produces perseverance. Let perseverance finish its work so that you may be mature and complete, not lacking anything.*" For leaders, these trials are not obstacles but opportunities to grow and emerge stronger.

At its heart, this book is all about transformation—transforming ourselves, our organizations, and even the world around us. Leaders who face the challenges of the valley with courage and humility create a lasting legacy that shines well beyond their immediate achievements. In every area of life—be it faith, politics, business, or community—the most remarkable leaders are those who uplift others to reach new heights by guiding them through the valleys with grace, resilience, and steadfast hope.

The Purpose of the Valley

Leadership is often seen as a journey to the top—a place filled with visibility, triumph, and influence. But the true heart of leadership isn't just found in the moments of success; it's also shaped in the valleys, those challenging low points that really test our character, resolve, and purpose. While the valley can be tough, it's also a fantastic opportunity for growth and a chance for leaders to show their impact on lives, organizations, and the world. Embracing the lessons of these valleys is essential for discovering a leader's true calling and lasting influence.

Purpose in Leadership Life

In leadership, having a sense of purpose means bringing our actions and decisions together in harmony with a larger mission or calling. It's that bright, inspiring vision that fuels and supports leaders, especially when times get tough. During challenging moments, when obstacles seem to surround us, purpose shines like a beacon of light, gently reminding leaders of the deeper "why" behind all their hard work. This clarity helps them persevere; it uplifts those they lead, encouraging everyone to remain strong in the face of difficulties.

A wonderful illustration of this can be found in the biblical story of Joseph. Although he faced daunting challenges—being sold into slavery by his brothers and wrongfully imprisoned—Joseph's journey didn't end in despair. His unwavering faith and deep understanding of his purpose helped him rise to become a leader in Egypt, where he played a pivotal role in saving many lives during a famine (Genesis 50:20). Joseph's experiences remind us that the tough times in our lives often prepare us for our true calling, helping us grow in resilience, humility, and wisdom along the way.

Leadership in the Valley

In the valley, leadership shines through by viewing challenges as wonderful opportunities for growth and transformation. These times peel back the layers of superficial motivations, uncovering the essence of a leader's character. It is during these tougher times that leaders truly learn to rely on their values, cultivate empathy, and sharpen their vision.

Take a moment to reflect on Malala Yousafzai, a true example of leadership forged through struggles in her valley. After bravely surviving an assassination attempt for advocating for girls' education, Malala emerged as a global symbol of resilience and determination. Her experiences in the valley sparked a powerful movement that touched the lives of millions around the world. Her journey demonstrates that the valley is not the final chapter; instead, it serves as an extraordinary starting point for creating a meaningful difference.

Biblical Insights on Purpose in the Valley

The Bible is rich with inspiring stories of leaders who found their purpose while navigating life's challenging valleys. Consider Moses; he spent forty years in the wilderness before guiding the Israelites out of Egypt. During this remarkable period, he cultivated humility and learned to lean on God, which equipped him for the monumental task that awaited him (Exodus 3:1-12). In Numbers 12:3, Moses is described as "a very humble man, more humble than anyone else on the face of the earth." This character trait, which was not evident in his pre-wilderness years, did not reflect weakness but rather a confident understanding of his place under the kingship of God. The wilderness was not merely a detour but a transformative season that shaped Moses into a leader who was both humbled and emboldened to act in obedience. Understanding our place in Christ does the same—it humbles us while empowering us to live in a way that honors God in everything.

Similarly, David's journey to the palace beautifully highlights the importance of welcoming the valley. Before ascending to the throne, David encountered many trials, including being hunted by King Saul. These challenges instilled patience, fostered dependence on God, and emphasized the need for integrity in leadership. In Psalm 23:4, David beautifully expresses his thoughts on these valleys: "Even though I walk through the darkest valley, I will fear no evil, for you are with me." This verse reflects the transformative power of the valley, a time when leaders deepen their trust in God and gather the strength they need to fulfill their vital purpose.

As we explore our purpose in the valley, leaders can also come to appreciate the incredible character and wisdom of God even more. I love the story of Elijah as a wonderful example of this idea. After witnessing a stunning victory against God's enemy, when fire rained down from heaven, Elijah unexpectedly found himself grappling with feelings of fear, depression, and anxiety. In 1 Kings 19:3, it says, "Elijah was afraid and ran for his life. When he reached Beersheba in Judah, he left his servant there and went a day's journey into the wilderness. There, he sat down under a broom bush and prayed that he might die."

The intimidating words of Queen Jezabel momentarily overshadowed Elijah's incredible triumph and his deep, meaningful connection with God. In this trying moment, Elijah found himself hiding and fleeing for his life, feeling overwhelmed and lost in a dark place of despair. However, it was during this challenging season that his "valley" led him to a profound lesson that would forever change his life.

The Lord said, "Go out and stand on the mountain in the presence of the Lord, for the Lord is about to pass by. Then, a mighty wind swept through, tearing the mountains apart and breaking the rocks apart before the Lord, but the Lord wasn't in the wind. After the wind, there was a mighty earthquake, yet again, the Lord was not in the earthquake. Then, following the earthquake, a fire appeared, but the Lord was not in the fire either. And after the fire, there came a gentle whisper. When Elijah heard this, he covered his face with his cloak and stepped out to stand at the entrance of the cave." (1 Kings 19:11-13)

Until that point, the Prophet had known God through powerful fire, miraculous events, and awe-inspiring moments. But this time brought something completely different; he met God in a way he never expected. The Lord spoke to him with a gentle whisper, revealing a beautiful new side of His character. This experience opened Elijah's eyes to see God in a fresh light. With this new understanding, he felt ready to embrace the next steps in God's incredible plan for his life, filled with clarity and renewed purpose.

In those challenging "valley" moments of our lives, God lovingly desires to work wonders within us. He gently guides us to a place where we might feel broken, helping us build a deeper reliance on Him. It's during these times that we experience growth and are shaped into the leaders and servants we're meant to become. This is when we can fully surrender, allowing ourselves to be lifted to the next beautiful mountaintop experience. While the valley can be painful and stretching, nothing is more rewarding than enduring through these seasons as they pave the way for us to achieve something greater for His purpose and glory.

Modern-Day Examples of Purposeful Leadership

In the business world, Indra Nooyi, the former CEO of PepsiCo, shines as a remarkable example of purposeful leadership rooted in her leadership values. Her journey to success was marked by numerous challenges, from navigating cultural differences to breaking barriers as a woman of color in a predominantly male industry. Nooyi was the first immigrant woman of color to run a Fortune 50 company, facing inherent challenges and stereotypes in a male-dominated industry. Nooyi's leadership truly stood out for her dedication to sustainable growth and social responsibility, transforming PepsiCo into a purpose-driven company that cares. Her inspiring path emphasizes how facing adversity can lead to impactful and transformative leadership.

In the world of nonprofits, Bryan Stevenson, an inspiring African American leader and founder of the Equal Justice Initiative, exemplifies the power of leading from the valley. His heartfelt passion for uplifting marginalized communities stems from a profound sense of community and purpose, cultivated through years of dedicated work focused on addressing deeply rooted societal injustices. Stevenson's unwavering commitment to defending those who have been wrongfully convicted, along with his brave fight against racial inequalities, shows how a genuine sense of purpose can help leaders overcome even the toughest challenges. Throughout his remarkable journey, Stevenson encountered various social hurdles, including persistent racism and a lack of support for his mission. Sadly, many held biases that led them to think innocent minorities should remain on death row in America.

The Valley as a Proving Ground

The valley is so much more than just a place of struggle; it's a unique proving ground where leaders truly discover their purpose and enhance their ability to inspire others. In these challenging moments, leaders cultivate empathy, resilience, and a clear vision that enables them to make a difference in people's lives and foster lasting change. By embracing the valuable lessons of the valley, leaders rise to the occasion, ready to navigate the often-complex responsibilities of their roles and amplify their influence.

As Paul beautifully expresses in Romans 5:3-4, *"Not only that, but we rejoice in our sufferings, knowing that suffering produces endurance, and endurance produces character, and character produces hope."* This hope, which springs from the valley, lays a solid foundation for leadership that goes beyond mere circumstances and genuinely transforms the world. Leaders who embrace the significance of the valley not only discover their true calling but also inspire others to embark on their own journeys, demonstrating that real leadership is crafted in the depths just as much as it is celebrated at greater heights.

Looking Ahead

Life's valley seasons are like hidden treasure chests, quietly bestowing upon us some of the most valuable lessons we could ever learn. These moments that we often overlook gently shape our character, refine our sense of purpose, and prepare us for the exciting journeys that lie ahead. While it's easy for the mountain peaks to grab our attention and make us feel as though that's where the real action is happening, it's really in the valleys where we discover the true strength to cultivate resilience, gain fresh perspectives, and gather the wisdom we need to navigate life's uncertainties. Yes, these seasons can sometimes feel lonely or discouraging, but they also overflow with remarkable opportunities for incredible growth and personal transformation.

As we turn the pages together to explore these invaluable lessons from our valley experiences, whether you're leading a vibrant church, managing a thriving business, or steering a nonprofit organization, remember that the insights I'll share are crafted just for you! They're designed to help you tackle those frustrating challenges, make wise decisions, and ultimately emerge even stronger on the other side of your trials. Together, we'll embark on an exciting journey to uncover effective strategies for overcoming obstacles, encouraging collaboration among your team, and staying true to your mission. This way, you'll feel fully equipped and ready for success, no matter what hurdles come your way. Let's get started!

Chapter 1

The Leader's Calling—More Than A Mountain

Understanding the Divine Purpose of Leadership

LEADERSHIP IS MORE THAN JUST AN ESTEEMED POSITION; it's truly a divine calling that invites us to nurture and guide those around us. Whether in business, ministry, or nonprofit organizations, genuine leaders carry the responsibility of influence. As Proverbs 29:18 reminds us, *"Where there is no vision, the people perish"* (KJV). This powerful verse illustrates the importance of leaders embracing their purpose with clarity and intention.

Dr. John C. Maxwell, a well-respected authority on leadership, shares that "It is not about titles, positions, or flowcharts. It is about one life influencing another." A real leader not only guides but also serves, mentors, and inspires others. This idea shows us that authentic leadership goes beyond mere authority, emphasizing how meaningful connections and support can significantly impact individuals. At its heart, the divine calling of leadership is all about stewardship, where leaders recognize their responsibility for the influence they have on others.

I remember when I was in my early twenties, a wonderful

leader in my church took me under his wing as a mentor. We spent several years working together in ministry, and I began to notice that he often avoided discussions about his education, credentials, and professional achievements. Whenever such topics arose, he would gently steer the conversation back to the heart of our mission—service, scripture, and our community. One day, I decided to ask him why, and his heartfelt response truly inspired me. He said, "John, I want all attention to be on Jesus and the people we serve. You never hear anyone who admires a beautiful house asking about the hammer or saw that built it." That moment opened my eyes to the genuine essence of authentic servant leadership.

For church leaders, this divine purpose offers a special perspective as they guide their congregations toward spiritual growth and fulfillment. Authentically leading a congregation encompasses much more than delivering sermons; it involves a heartfelt commitment to offering spiritual guidance and support to individuals within the community. Church leaders need to be sensitive to the diverse needs of their congregation, providing counseling, mentorship, and resources that enrich their spiritual journeys. Moreover, these leaders play a vital role in building a sense of community, and inspiring members to engage in outreach and service projects that embody Christ-like love and compassion. With their positive influence, church leaders have a wonderful ability and opportunity to inspire faith that nurtures a deep sense of purpose and belonging for everyone in the congregation.

This lesson in humility and servant leadership extends beyond ministry—it holds profound significance in the world of business as well. Just as my mentor emphasized shifting the focus away from himself and onto the greater mission, successful business owners understand that true leadership is not about personal accolades but about fostering purpose, integrity, and innovation.

For business owners, embracing a sense of purpose and understanding authentic leadership is truly a meaningful journey. It involves the heartfelt responsibility of cultivating a culture filled with integrity and innovation. Integrity serves as the foundation of trust, helping to ensure that business practices are both ethical and sustainable. When businesses prioritize honesty and uphold strong ethical standards, they enhance their reputation and also build lasting relationships with customers and employees alike. At the same time, innovation empowers these businesses to stay competitive and adapt quickly in a rapidly changing marketplace. By fostering creativity and looking ahead, business owners can cultivate a lively environment that attracts customers and nurtures loyalty for long-term success.

This simple yet essential principle brings to mind a story about a business owner in New York City. Mrs. Ramos ran a family-owned coffee shop famous for its inviting atmosphere, Puerto Rican dishes, and outstanding service. One day, she received a delivery of dry beans that, upon inspection, fell short of the high-quality standards she had promised her customers. Instead of using them to cut costs, she promptly reached out to her supplier and notified her customers that she would temporarily offer a different menu until the matter was resolved. Her honesty struck a chord with the community, and rather than suffering a loss of business, her devoted customers valued her openness and dedication to quality. News of her integrity circulated, drawing in additional local visitors who appreciated businesses prioritizing ethics over earnings. Eventually, Mrs. Ramos' coffee shop evolved into a cherished fixture, celebrated not only for its delicious food but also for the trust it built with every customer who entered.

Moses: Called in the Wilderness

I really enjoy the story of Moses. It wonderfully demonstrates that leadership can often emerge from the most
surprising places. In Exodus chapter 3, Moses has a profound
encounter with God through the burning bush. In this pivotal
moment, God calls Moses to guide the Israelites out of Egypt.
Even though Moses feels hesitant and questions, *"Who am I
that I should go to Pharaoh?"* (Exodus 3:11), God tenderly reas-
sures him, saying, *"I will be with you"* (Exodus 3:12). Isn't it
fascinating that Moses' calling didn't emerge from the grand
palace where he once held a place amongst royalty, nor did it
happen before an audience of thousands, but rather it blos-
somed in the quiet serenity of the wilderness, in his own private
valley? This powerful lesson teaches us that true leadership is
often forged in moments of obscurity and shaped through life's
challenges. The wilderness symbolizes a time of preparation—a
season where God refines our character, strengthens our
resilience, and helps clarify our purpose.

Leaders across all areas of life may find themselves in their
own "wilderness" moments. For business owners, this could be a
challenging period of financial uncertainty. Church leaders
might face the hurdles of declining attendance or spiritual difficulties. Nonprofit leaders may grapple with limited resources or
increasing demands. Just like Moses, it's essential for leaders to
trust that their calling is deeply rooted in God's purpose,
offering them strength and guidance along the way.

Reconnecting with Your Calling in the Valley

Life's valleys are not just times of struggle; they're
wonderful opportunities for growth and reflection. As Psalm
23:4 beautifully states, *"Even though I walk through the valley*

of the shadow of death, I will fear no evil, for you are with me." During these seasons, leaders have the chance to reconnect with their calling and refine their vision. Take Nehemiah, for example, who faced challenges while rebuilding the walls of Jerusalem. In Nehemiah 2:17, we hear his inspiring words: *"Come, let us rebuild the wall of Jerusalem, and we will no longer be in disgrace."* Nehemiah's leadership was rooted in his commitment to fulfilling God's purpose, no matter the obstacles he faced. His unwavering faith inspired those around him to join in the mission, creating a sense of community and shared vision. With their spirits high, they faced challenges together, showing how the strength of teamwork can bring about meaningful change.

Leadership expert Simon Sinek masterfully highlights that, *"Working hard for something we don't care about is called stress; working hard for something we love is called passion."* When leaders embrace their passion, they uncover a wonderful sense of purpose. This heartfelt connection helps them to navigate challenges with greater ease. Their enthusiasm becomes contagious, encouraging others to look at their own motivations. By sharing their journey openly, leaders can foster a warm environment of support. Together, they can triumph over obstacles and reach their shared goals.

For leaders in business, these valleys offer an excellent opportunity to pause and rethink their operations, helping them align more closely with God's vision for their businesses. For further insight into Christ-centered leadership in business, I highly recommend *Afraid to Trust* by Peter Demos. His journey of coming to faith and embracing God as the CEO of his business is truly inspiring. Demos' story serves as a powerful reminder that faith and integrity can transform a business and the lives of those it impacts. Similarly, church leaders can use these moments to seek God's loving guidance for their congrega-

Between Mountains

tion. Nonprofit leaders, on the other hand, can reconnect with their mission by shifting their focus back to the amazing people they serve rather than getting bogged down by the challenges that lie ahead of them.

Practical Insight: Rediscovering Your Purpose

Finding our purpose again is vital for nurturing strong leadership. Here are practical steps for leaders to realign with their calling:

1. Reflect on Your Why - Leadership begins with understanding your "why." In Luke 19:10, Jesus states His purpose clearly: *"For the Son of Man came to seek and to save the lost."* Leaders should regularly reflect on their motivation and divine purpose.
2. Seek God in Prayer - James 1:5 encourages us: *"If any of you lacks wisdom, you should ask God, who gives generously to all without finding fault."* Prayer is vital for gaining clarity and direction.
3. Engage Trusted Mentors - Proverbs 15:22 advises, *"Plans fail for lack of counsel, but with many advisers they succeed."* Leaders should surround themselves with wise mentors who can provide healthy perspectives and challenge us to turn our plans and ideas over to God to change as needed.
4. Take Practical Steps of Faith - Hebrews 11:1 defines faith as *"confidence in what we hope for and assurance about what we do not see."* Leaders must take actionable steps toward the vision God has given them, even in uncertainty.

6

For business leaders, this might involve revisiting their business plans and seeking new opportunities. Church leaders can engage their congregation or board of directors in a visioning process to rediscover their mission. Nonprofit leaders can focus on celebrating the impact of their work to reignite passion among staff and other stakeholders.

Summary

Leadership is about so much more than just big celebratory moments. It's really about the journey we take through the valleys of our lives. These valleys can bring unique challenges and hardships, and it's through navigating them that a leader's true character and effectiveness really shine. Take great leaders like Moses, for example, who journeyed through the wilderness, and Nehemiah, who faced numerous challenges while working to rebuild Jerusalem. Their stories remind us that it's often during tough times that leaders find their voice and true purpose. Through these experiences, they build resilience, gain wisdom, and learn how to inspire others—even when the road is tough. These valleys aren't just struggles; they are beautiful places of growth where leaders nurture the qualities necessary for leading with empathy and vision.

Understanding the divine purpose of leadership can truly transform one's ability to make a meaningful impact. It's important for leaders to reconnect with their original calling and draw insights that can inspire practical actions. This process often involves self-reflection and a strong commitment to personal growth, along with a genuine openness to learn from past experience. By celebrating their unique journeys and the critical lessons learned along the way, leaders can genuinely embrace these insights to strengthen their impact within their communities and beyond. When leaders are in harmony with their God-given purpose and empowered by the knowledge they've gained, they naturally inspire and uplift others, cultivating a sense of community and shared vision that genuinely resonates with those they serve.

This perspective is especially vital for business owners dedicated to building ethical enterprises, church leaders guiding their congregations, and nonprofit leaders addressing urgent societal needs. When leadership aligns with God's purpose, it becomes a remarkable force for positive change, impacting lives, organizations, and the world in profound ways. As leaders answer their calling, they carry out their divine purpose, spreading hope, transforming lives, and creating lasting impact.

Chapter 2

Humility - The Soil of Spiritual Leadership

The Necessity of Humility in Leadership

HUMILITY SERVES AS THE CORNERSTONE OF SPIRITUAL leadership, forming a solid foundation for influence, wisdom, and grace. It's important to recognize that humility is not a weakness; instead, it is a reflection of strong character and a heartfelt commitment to prioritizing others. C.S. Lewis beautifully said, *"Humility is not thinking less of yourself, but thinking of yourself less."*

Back in the early 2000s, I had the wonderful opportunity to work for a Christian radio network in New York City. In this role, I collaborated with local pastors who were eager to start their own broadcast ministries with a desire to share their message of hope. I also had the opportunity to work alongside pastors who, over the years, had developed successful nationwide radio ministries. It was such a rewarding experience to engage with both large and small ministries. I met well-known pastors, some of whom might be seen as 'celebrities,' as well as those cherished solely by their local congregations. Throughout it all, I found leaders wholly driven by humble, Christlike values

9

and motivations. These incredible individuals left a lasting impression on my life. They weren't focused on gaining attention but on spreading the powerful message of the Gospel through their broadcasts. Their true ambition came from a desire to create a legacy of transformation rather than fame and affluence. So many of these wonderful, down-to-earth pastors and ministers, who are deeply committed to Christ, have truly inspired my journey just by the way they live out their dedication to serving both Christ and others.

In those valley seasons—those challenging times filled with the mundane, struggles, uncertainty, or adversity—humility takes on even greater significance. It empowers leaders to recognize their limitations and bravely seek help from others, creating a warm atmosphere of shared support and resilience. Humble leaders choose to let go of pride and the urge to control everything; they are more receptive to listening and learning from those around them, which naturally fosters deeper empathy and understanding.

In these challenging times, embracing humility opens up incredible opportunities for collaboration, fresh ideas, and genuine connections. By prioritizing others, leaders can inspire their teams to unite, turning obstacles into chances for growth and unity. Ultimately, humility not only boosts a leader's influence but also lays a strong foundation for navigating the complexities of leadership, especially during the toughest times.

When leaders tackle challenges humbly, they foster an atmosphere where team members feel appreciated and listened to, resulting in stronger relationships and alliances that enable all parts of the team to function effectively. Additionally, humility allows leaders to learn from their mistakes and adapt their strategies, which is essential for growth and success in any organization.

The Apostle Paul captures the essence of humility in

Philippians 2:3–4: *"Do nothing out of selfish ambition or vain conceit. Instead, in humility value others above yourselves, not looking to your own interests but each of you to the interests of the others."* This timeless principle can influence leaders in business, ministry, and nonprofit sectors to bring out the best in each of them.

Abraham Lincoln epitomized humility during his presidency. In spite of his numerous achievements, Lincoln once expressed, "I have been driven many times to my knees by the overwhelming conviction that I had nowhere else to go." His trust in a higher power and dedication to service over self-interest truly reflect the biblical understanding of humility as a vital part of godly leadership.

For business leaders, humility fosters collaboration and innovation. Church leaders embody humility by serving their congregations rather than seeking personal recognition. Nonprofit leaders demonstrate humility by prioritizing mission and people over organizational prestige.

Biblical Examples: David and Jesus

David: Humility in Adversity

David's journey to kingship reflects the essence of humility. Before stepping onto the throne, David had several chances to harm King Saul, who was intent on taking his life. But when David has the opportunity to kill Saul, in 1 Samuel 24:4–6, David chooses not to, saying, *"The Lord forbid that I should do such a thing to my master, the Lord's anointed."* This restraint showcases David's respect for God's timing and authority.

Throughout his reign, David's humility continued to shine. In 2 Samuel 7:18, he prays, *"Who am I, Sovereign Lord, and what is my family, that you have brought me this far?"* His heartfelt gratitude and recognition of God's provision remind us that true humility springs from a place of dependence and thankfulness. This isn't weakness; it's a profound testament to enduring strength.

Another compelling example of David's humility and trust in God's sovereignty is found in 2 Samuel 16:5–13. As King David fled from his son Absalom, Shimei, a man from Saul's household, hurled curses and stones at him and his men. Abishai, one of David's soldiers, wanted to kill Shimei in retaliation, but David intervened, responding with remarkable restraint.

In 2 Samuel 16:10-11 (NIV), David said, *"What does this have to do with you, you sons of Zeruiah? If he is cursing because the Lord said to him, 'Curse David,' who can ask, 'Why do you do this?'... Leave him alone; let him curse, for the Lord has told him to."* Instead of seeking revenge, David acknowledged that even this hardship might be part of God's plan. His response is a powerful demonstration of grace, humility, and unwavering trust in God's greater purpose.

Jesus: The Ultimate Model of Humility

Jesus shows His humility through His incarnation and earthly ministry. Philippians 2:5–8 (ESV) wonderfully captures this idea: *"Have this mind among yourselves, which is yours in Christ Jesus, who, though he was in the form of God, did not count equality with God a thing to be grasped, but emptied himself, by taking the form of a servant."* Jesus' act of washing his disciples' feet in John 13 is another poignant example of humility. He encourages them, saying, *"Now that I, your Lord and Teacher, have washed your feet, you also should wash one another's feet"* (John 13:14). Jesus shows us that true greatness isn't just about power or status; it's really about how we serve and uplift others. This beautiful idea is grounded in love and compassion for everyone around us, and it's such an important principle for leaders to embrace, especially in today's world.

Humility in the Valley: A Leader's Secret Strength

The valley—often symbolizing those metaphorical low points—is a special place where humility can blossom. These experiences encourage leaders to face their limitations and lean on others, as well as on God. John C. Maxwell notes, *"True leadership must be for the benefit of the followers, not to enrich the leader."* Embracing humility allows leaders to focus on serving their teams instead of pursuing self-promotion, personal gain, and pleasure.

Biblical leaders frequently navigated through valleys that significantly shaped their character and leadership skills. For instance, Joseph faced betrayal and imprisonment but emerged as a remarkable leader who saved nations, demonstrating incredible humility through forgiveness and a strategic vision (Genesis 50:20). Similarly, Moses developed humility during his time in the wilderness before leading the Israelites. Numbers 12:3 tells us he was *"more humble than anyone else on the face of the earth."*

For business leaders, these valleys might include ethical hurdles or team conflicts. Church leaders may encounter challenges such as declining attendance or disagreements within the community, and these moments require a humble heart to listen, adapt, and seek God's guidance. Nonprofit leaders often encounter resource limitations, which requires humility to listen, learn, inspire their teams, and drive innovative solutions.

Practical Insight: Cultivating Humility Through Service

Humility isn't something we're born with; it's something we develop through heartfelt and consistent effort. One way to nurture humility is through servant leadership, which involves prioritizing the needs of others over our own. In Matthew 20:26–28, Jesus highlights this idea: *"Whoever wants to become great among you must be your servant, and whoever wants to be first must be your slave—just as the Son of Man did not come to be served, but to serve."*

Practical strategies for cultivating humility include:

1. **Listening Actively:** Leaders who listen demonstrate respect and value for others' perspectives.
2. **Delegating and Empowering:** Entrusting others with responsibility builds trust and fosters shared growth.
3. **Seeking Feedback:** Soliciting honest input fosters accountability and self-awareness.

In his book, Mere Christianity, C.S. Lewis introduced a wonderful teaching that is often summarized and quoted today in the following manner: *"Humility isn't thinking less of yourself, but rather thinking about yourself less and others more."* This perspective encourages business leaders to empower their employees to share their ideas and talents. Similarly, church leaders cultivate humility by placing the spiritual growth of their congregations at the forefront. Nonprofit leaders embody humility when they advocate for their cause, focusing on the mission rather than personal recognition or accolades.

Summary

Humility represents strength and character rather than weakness. It's an essential quality that helps leaders navigate the many challenges they face in diverse settings like business, spiritual spaces, or nonprofit organizations. A humble leader embraces their limitations and welcomes input from others, encouraging a collaborative and open atmosphere. This heartwarming willingness to serve over personal ambition builds trust and respect among team members. By staying true to their values and purpose, humble leaders create a culture that promotes both personal and professional growth for everyone involved.

Humility is also a cornerstone of effective leadership and serves as a catalyst for transformative change within organizations. When leaders embrace humility, they prioritize the wellbeing and aspirations of their team members. This approach fosters a culture of inclusivity and collaboration and also encourages open communication. Team members who feel valued and understood are more likely to contribute creatively and energetically to their work. Humble leaders are skilled at recognizing the potential of others and empowering their teams to strive for personal and collective excellence. As a result, the organization benefits from heightened morale and productivity, as employees feel inspired to work towards a common goal, knowing they are supported and esteemed.

Moreover, the influence of humble leadership extends beyond immediate workplace dynamics; it cultivates a robust community that enhances individual experiences and wellbeing. When leaders genuinely demonstrate care and concern for their followers, they establish deep, trusting relationships that promote a sense of belonging. This connection boosts team dynamics and creates a wonderful legacy of positivity and support that can inspire future generations. When leaders model humility, they become change agents who nurture resilience, empathy, and understanding, helping to create an inspiring environment. The influence of such leadership paves the way for a brighter future, where everyone feels fulfilled not just in their careers but in their personal lives as well, leading to vibrant communities and enriched lives.

Chapter 3

Perseverance - The Valley of Strength

The Power of Perseverance in Leadership

PERSEVERANCE SHINES AS A KEY TRAIT OF EXCEPTIONAL leadership. It's all about holding firm in the face of difficulties or delays on the journey to success. While some leaders may only make a temporary impact, those who embrace perseverance create lasting change. This isn't about merely hanging on; it's an energetic and determined quest for purpose, fueled by a strong vision and a firm belief in what lies ahead. As Winston Churchill once said, *"Success is not final, failure is not fatal: it is the courage to continue that counts."* It's this very courage that shapes our character, lifts up our teams, and nurtures resilience throughout our organizations.

In the early days of my leadership journey, I often struggled to persevere. Whenever something became too much of a challenge, I would often find myself raising a white flag, eager to find the nearest exit. I would retreat and conceal myself, though the people around me likely didn't notice this behavior. You might wonder how that works—well, I kept my struggles quietly tucked away in my heart and mind. I would allow time to help me craft a way to escape without making a scene. Honestly, I'm not proud of that chapter in my life. But I'm grateful that I've grown resilient and ready to face the valleys head-on. After spending several seasons in the valley, I've learned to lean on God and trust my instincts as a leader. The valley has become my terrain for growth and refinement. While I don't look forward to the valleys, I genuinely value the lessons from each arduous experience. I've embraced a new motto as a leader that feels both simple and weighty: "It's always too soon to give up!"

So, how does all this apply to your business, work, church, or nonprofit? Well, leaders often encounter significant hurdles like limited resources, small teams, and unexpected challenges – to name a few. It's perseverance that allows leaders to tackle such obstacles with grace and determination, encouraging your teams to move forward with confidence toward your shared vision. John Quincy Adams put it clearly when he said, *"Patience and perseverance have a magical effect before which difficulties disappear and obstacles vanish."* Indeed, perseverance in leadership acts as a guiding light, illuminating the path for others even through the darkest moments.

James 1: Building Resilience Through Trials

In James 1:2-4, we read, *"Consider it pure joy, my brothers and sisters, whenever you face trials of many kinds, because you know that the testing of your faith produces perseverance. Let perseverance finish its work so that you may be mature and complete, not lacking anything."* These verses remind us that the challenges we encounter aren't just hurdles to overcome; they are precious opportunities for both personal and professional growth. Each trial faced opens the door to a better under-standing of oneself and helps develop essential skills. By embracing these challenges instead of avoiding them, we can experience significant growth in our character and abilities, leading to a more resilient and effective leadership style.

Business owners often navigate significant challenges, from struggling to find trustworthy employees to dealing with rising insurance costs. Many also face the pressure of dealing with demanding customers who expect more than what is reasonable, sometimes resorting to threats of bad reviews or even attempts to "cancel" the business if their expectations aren't met. These trials can be discouraging and overwhelming, testing both resilience and integrity, yet they also present opportunities to stand firm in ethical values and emerge stronger on the other side. By seeing these trials as opportunities for growth, you can spark innovation and creativity within your teams. Similarly, church leaders might face declining membership or some internal disagreements, but staying strong in the faith can indeed breathe new life into their ministry. Nonprofit leaders, often working with tight budgets and facing big societal needs, can feel empowered knowing that perseverance will lead to lasting positive change.

Leadership Lessons from Job and Paul

Let's look at figures from the Old and New Testament, Job and Paul, who effectively illustrate the significance of perseverance during life's trials. Job, described as *"blameless and upright"* (Job 1:1), faced unimaginable suffering, losing his wealth, family, and health. Yet, through it all, he remained steadfast in his faith, proclaiming, *"Though he slay me, yet will I hope in him"* (Job 13:15). His story reminds all leaders that perseverance often involves embracing God's purpose and sovereignty even during those tough moments when everything feels a bit overwhelming and uncertain.

Paul, the Apostle, encountered relentless trials—shipwrecks, imprisonments, and opposition. Yet, he kept moving forward, notably expressing, *"I press on toward the goal to win the prize for which God has called me heavenward in Christ Jesus"* (Philippians 3:14). Paul's life illustrates perseverance, driven by a clear vision and a profound sense of calling.

For today's leaders, these inspiring stories offer timeless wisdom. Business owners can find strength in Job's endurance during the loss of trusted stakeholders and partners, while nonprofit leaders can draw motivation from Paul's unwavering pursuit of his mission, even in tough times when few people are willing to serve and sacrifice their time in support of a worthwhile cause. Church leaders, navigating cultural and societal shifts, can draw encouragement from Paul's steadfast commitment to his divine calling.

Perseverance: Not Passivity but Strength of Character and Vision

Perseverance is often seen simply as basic willpower, but it's so much more than that! True perseverance means actively and intentionally working towards our goals, even when we encounter obstacles or setbacks. It's all about staying committed, keeping our focus, and finding the motivation to push through challenges, no matter how tough they may be. This essential quality demonstrates our determination and reveals our resilience and the spirit to persevere, which is crucial in our journey toward success. In her inspiring book, Grit: The Power of Passion and Perseverance, leadership expert Angela Duckworth shares that perseverance is really about blending passion with consistent effort over time. She notes in her book, "Enthusiasm is common. Endurance is rare." It's this remarkable endurance that sets apart those leaders who truly make a lasting impact.

Christian thinker Dallas Willard once shared, *"The most important thing in your life is not what you do; it's who you become."* Perseverance plays a vital role in shaping the character of leaders, transforming them into inspiring individuals who uplift and motivate others. It also requires a clear vision, as leaders without direction often struggle to navigate hardships with a sense of purpose and stability.

Consider Mother Teresa's inspiring example. Her unwavering commitment to helping the most vulnerable in Calcutta, despite facing numerous challenges, exemplifies the powerful impact of perseverance in nonprofit leadership. This idea conveys the notion that perseverance transcends mere endurance; it represents an engaging journey toward a profound purpose.

Practical Insight: Embracing Challenges as Opportunities for Growth

Leaders in all sectors can cultivate perseverance by embracing challenges as opportunities for growth. Here are practical steps to develop this vital trait:

1. **Reframe Challenges:** View obstacles as opportunities for innovation and growth. Adopt a mindset that sees trials as stepping stones to success.
2. **Build a Support System:** Surround yourself with mentors, peers, and a team that shares your vision and provides encouragement during tough times.
3. **Anchor Yourself in Vision and Faith:** A clear vision and faith in God's purpose provide the strength to endure. Proverbs 29:18 reminds us, *"Where there is no vision, the people perish."*

Leaders must consistently revisit their "why" to remain motivated.

4. **Develop Resilience Through Practice:** Engage in activities that stretch your endurance, such as setting challenging but achievable goals and reflecting on lessons learned from setbacks.

5. **Lead by Example:** Demonstrate perseverance in your actions, inspiring your team to adopt a similar attitude. As John Quincy Adams noted, *"If your actions inspire others to dream more, learn more, do more and become more, you are a leader."*

Business leaders can leverage market disruptions to pivot and explore new partnership opportunities. Church leaders should view decreasing attendance not merely as a challenge but as an opportunity to invest more meaningfully in those who remain. By concentrating on intentional discipleship and mentorship, they can empower and strengthen these individuals, ultimately equipping them to share the Gospel with enthusiasm and understanding. Nonprofit leaders can maximize limited resources and tap into community and human assets to create innovative solutions and partnerships.

Summary

Perseverance is a catalyst for transformation; it enables individuals and leaders to turn daunting challenges into meaningful milestones. When faced with obstacles—be it in a business, a religious community, or a nonprofit initiative—the ability to keep going sets influential leaders apart. These leaders foster a culture of resilience in their teams, inspiring members to embrace challenges instead of retreating from them. By showcasing persistence, they cultivate a mindset that sees setbacks not as failures but as stepping stones that lead to personal and collective growth. This uplifting approach nurtures an environment where innovation flourishes, and everyone feels empowered to take risks while pursuing their goals.

Additionally, the biblical perspective on perseverance, as highlighted in James 1:12, emphasizes its spiritual importance. The promise of a 'crown of life' for those who endure trials reminds us that perseverance isn't just about finding success here on Earth; it's also about growing our character and faith through tough times. It's all about embracing a lasting perspective that goes beyond our time here. As we embrace this wisdom, we can motivate those in our communities to adopt a similar viewpoint, encouraging them to see struggles as opportunities for growth. By grounding our resolve in our beliefs, we strengthen ourselves and uplift those around us, creating a path for profound and lasting impact in our respective spheres of influence.

Chapter 4

Vision – The Eyes Of Faith In The Valley

The Importance of Vision in Leadership

LEADERSHIP INSPIRES AND GUIDES OTHERS TOWARD A shared dream. At its core, effective leadership thrives on faith—not just in a religious way, but as a deep belief in one's vision and the promise of future success. This kind of faith works like magic, allowing us to see opportunities that might be missed by others. With a strong sense of faith, we can tackle challenges more effectively, build resilience, and boost our teams' confidence. Holding firm with unwavering belief helps us push through obstacles and rally everyone to work together in pursuit of ambitious goals. By doing this, we nurture a culture of hope and possibility that resonates within our organizations.

Proverbs 29:18 highlights the importance of vision in leadership, *"Where there is no vision, the people perish."* A strong, inspiring vision not only propels a leader forward but also acts as a guiding light for their followers. Visionary leaders have a special talent for sharing their dreams in a way that motivates those around them; they create a vivid picture of a brighter future that lifts the spirits of their team. As I consider this topic,

I am reminded of George Snyman, the founder of Hands at Work in Africa—a humble and compassionate man from South Africa. For years, he and his wife were busy professionals, living as Sunday Christians, believing they had little more to give. However, when God called him to deepen his faith, he accepted an invitation to serve in a local ministry. This led him to a nearby community devastated by poverty and the AIDS epidemic, where he realized he had far more to offer than he had imagined. As God continued to lead him, George emerged as a visionary leader, inspiring others with his deep love for the people he served and his unwavering faith. Today, Hands at Work has expanded across the world, drawing many to join in its mission of care and compassion.

This strong bond around a vision cultivates loyalty and commitment, making team members feel essential to a larger mission. In a world that is constantly changing, with uncertainty often around the corner, such leaders play a vital role—they share an uplifting narrative that fosters collaboration and inno-vation, encouraging everyone to work together toward the shared vision.

As I look back on my journey, I am filled with immense grat-itude for the incredible visionary leaders who have shaped my growth and inspired me along the way. Their steadfast beliefs, clear visions, and warm personal touch have taught me the importance of building connections with others. Today, I strive to bring that same vital energy into my work, with a strong focus on uplifting and motivating my teams, clients, and mentees, just as my mentors uplifted me at the start of my journey. I truly believe that when we foster a positive and supportive environ-ment, we can accomplish incredible things together. It's about establishing meaningful connections, encouraging one another to pursue our dreams, and celebrating every victory, big and small. My goal is to foster an atmosphere where everyone feels valued, heard, and inspired to reach their fullest potential. By working together, we can overcome challenges, gain insights from our experiences, and ensure that this journey is not only productive but also enjoyable. The excitement of seeing what we can accomplish as a team keeps me motivated every single day.

In short, visionary leadership stems from a deep-seated belief—an inspiring confidence in the possibilities of transformation and ongoing growth. John Maxwell, who is highly regarded as a leader in Christian thought, captures this sentiment in his assertion: *"A leader is one who knows the way, goes the way, and shows the way."* This insightful perspective inspires and empowers leaders, enabling them to navigate a pathway that aligns their mission with a deep and enduring purpose and acts as a compass when faced with challenges. This principle is not confined to the realms of corporate boardrooms; it resonates equally in the mission statements of nonprofits and in the spiritual guidance provided by churches. In essence, visionary leadership transcends specific contexts, embodying a universal approach that encourages those in positions of influence to pursue their goals with integrity and a clear sense of direction, fostering environments that nurture growth and development in all stakeholders involved.

Seeing Beyond the Present Struggle

Faith allows leaders to see beyond the challenges and obstacles they face, helping them envision a brighter future. This uplifting perspective is critical during difficult times. The apostle Paul aptly illustrates this idea in 2 Corinthians 4:18: *"So we fix our eyes not on what is seen, but on what is unseen since what is seen is temporary, but what is unseen is eternal."* Paul's encouraging words inspire leaders to keep their eyes on the ultimate goal and not to be discouraged by temporary setbacks. He further builds on this thought in Colossians 3:2, encouraging us to *"Set your minds on things that are above, not on things that are on earth."* This perspective is our pathway to growth and forward movement through life's valleys. It helps us to keep hope alive and stay in harmony with what truly matters – God's amazing plan.

For business owners, faith often shines through as the courage to invest in innovative ideas, even when financial risks are involved. For church leaders, it means placing trust in God's plan while skillfully handling the challenges their congregations face. In the nonprofit world, faith becomes a powerful motivator for pursuing those ambitious dreams that might seem just out of reach. It's this unwavering faith that empowers leaders to stay committed to their vision, even when the path ahead feels daunting.

Historical leaders like Martin Luther King Jr. demonstrated the remarkable power of a faith-driven vision. King's legendary "I Have a Dream" speech brilliantly expressed a hopeful outlook rooted in belief and determination, encouraging countless individuals to rise above racial injustice and strive for a brighter future filled with equality and unity. King famously said, *"Faith is taking the first step even when you don't see the whole staircase,"* capturing the essence of leadership driven by a compelling vision.

Habakkuk's Vision for the Future

The prophet Habakkuk presents a thought-provoking biblical example of faith-driven vision. In Habakkuk 2:2-3, the Lord kindly instructs, *"Write the vision; make it plain on tablets, so he may run who reads it. For still the vision awaits its appointed time; it hastens to the end—it will not lie. If it seems slow, wait for it; it will surely come; it will not delay."*

Habakkuk's vision emphasizes the importance of patience, persistence, and clarity. Leaders are encouraged to articulate their vision clearly and to trust in its fulfillment, even when it takes time. This journey may have its bumps, but staying focused on the ultimate goal can lead to incredible outcomes. Remember, every great endeavor requires time, and nurturing your vision will make the rewards even sweeter.

For business leaders, this could mean setting thoughtful strategic goals and embracing the journey of incremental growth. This idea is supported by Proverbs 3:5-6: "Trust in the Lord with all your heart, and do not lean on your own understanding. In all your ways acknowledge him, and he will make straight your paths." For church leaders, it might involve casting an inspiring vision for community impact and faithfully managing resources to make it happen under the guidance of the Holy Spirit. Nonprofit leaders can also find assurance in Habakkuk's message that with faithful perseverance, results will follow.

Practical Insight: Keeping Your Vision Alive in Difficult Seasons

Nurturing a faith-driven vision requires heartfelt effort and perseverance, especially during challenging times. It's crucial for leaders to regularly share their vision with their teams, reminding everyone of its significance and importance. I recommend doing this at least annually, preferably two or three times, to ensure that all team members, including newcomers, remain focused and engaged throughout the year.

Helen Keller shared a profound insight when she said, *"The only thing worse than being blind is having sight but no vision."*

That certainly gives us something to ponder! Without a clear vision, leaders might feel stuck in their journey, but those who nurture their vision can ignite resilience and inspire creativity in those around them.

Practical strategies for maintaining vision include:

1. *Regular Reflection*: Leaders should periodically revisit their mission and goals, ensuring alignment with their core values and faith foundation.
2. *Team Collaboration*: Sharing the vision with others and seeking their input fosters a sense of collective ownership and accountability.
3. *Adaptability*: Although the core vision remains constant, strategies for achieving it may need to be adjusted in response to changing circumstances. This flexibility demonstrates a leader's strength of character and commitment to the vision.
4. *Faith in Action*: Leaders should model faith through their actions, showing trust in the process and the people they lead. This inspires confidence and perseverance among their teams.

Application for Business, Church, and Nonprofit Leaders

For business leaders, embracing a faith-driven vision means setting ambitious goals and trusting their ability to adapt and innovate. Take Sara Blakely, the founder of Spanx, as an inspiring example. She held firm to her vision of revolutionizing women's shapewear, and even when faced with rejection from numerous manufacturers, she didn't give up on her dream. Her unwavering faith in her idea helped turn Spanx into a billion-dollar success, empowering women and reshaping an entire industry.

Church leaders can find motivation in the story of biblical figures like Nehemiah, who faced challenges while rebuilding Jerusalem's walls, all driven by a vision deeply rooted in faith. Nehemiah's journey teaches us about the power of prayer, thoughtful planning, and persistence when fulfilling a God-given vision.

Nonprofit leaders can also draw inspiration from individuals like Scott Harrison, the founder of charity: water. His vision and unwavering commitment to providing clean water access have transformed the lives of millions in underserved communities around the world. Harrison's leadership exemplifies how a deep-seated faith in humanity and a dedication to advocacy can drive systemic change and unite diverse communities in meaningful ways.

Summary

Faith is so much more than just a passive belief; it actively shapes the heart of visionary leadership! It empowers leaders to rise above immediate challenges and envision a greater purpose that truly inspires their teams and stakeholders. When leaders ground their aspirations in faith, they create a bountiful culture of trust and resilience—two essential ingredients for any successful endeavor. This trust energizes their followers and builds a solid foundation from which innovative ideas can sprout. In this way, faith becomes a driving force that encourages leaders to take bold actions even in uncertain times, nurturing an atmosphere rich in growth and creativity. Additionally, faith brings team members closer together, nurturing a culture of collaboration and support. It inspires leaders to be their authentic selves and embrace vulnerability, fostering deeper connections with their team. This heartfelt bond ultimately cultivates a shared vision, uniting everyone around common goals and dreams.

It's clear that leaders who cultivate their faith are much better prepared to tackle challenges and stay true to their mission, believing that their efforts will eventually bear fruit. Whether leading a business, a church, or a nonprofit, big or small, those who incorporate faith into their leadership approach will be able to face difficulties with both grace and determination. These incredible leaders will make a lasting difference and create a legacy that touches lives well beyond their immediate community, inspiring everyone they encounter.

Chapter 5

Leading With Compassion—The Shepherd's Heart

COMPASSIONATE LEADERSHIP IS A BEAUTIFUL AND VITAL quality that resonates well with people across all kinds of organizations. When leaders embody compassion, they create meaningful connections with those they serve and guide, fostering an environment of trust, loyalty, and mutual respect. It's not just about being kind or showing empathy when it's easy; true compassionate leadership weaves these values into every decision, action, and relationship. In this chapter, we'll journey through the importance of compassion in leadership, shining a light on the inspiring example of Jesus as the Good Shepherd. We'll explore how compassion is lived out through genuine care and empathy, especially with challenging people or those moments we all dread.

The Role of Compassion in Leadership

Compassion is not just a Christ-like virtue; it's a crucial part of what makes leadership effective. It helps leaders genuinely connect with their teams, communities, and those they serve. At its core, compassion shows our understanding of the struggles and challenges others face. This understanding inspires us to take meaningful actions to lighten their loads and enhance their well-being. Unlike pity, which can feel cold and distant, compassion offers a warm invitation to connect with one another on a deeper level. It heightens our awareness of others' struggles and allows us to share in their emotions and experiences. By embracing compassion, we're motivated to take action —rather than just feel—which can bring about real support and positive change in someone's life. This sense of interconnectedness not only enriches our relationships but fosters a vibrant community and a sense of belonging for everyone involved.

Compassion marries empathy—our heartfelt ability to feel and connect with the emotional experiences of those around us —with a proactive spirit. Compassion, as Christ modeled it, invites us to reach out and help those who are struggling.

When we open ourselves up to the experiences of others, we discover countless ways to offer a helping hand, reflecting the spirit of compassion. This appears in many forms: being a great listener, volunteering our time for community projects, or sharing valuable resources with those who need them the most. Ultimately, compassion not only helps us build stronger relationships but also creates a ripple effect of hope that uplifts individuals facing challenges and nurtures more resilient and supportive communities all around us.

Scripture Reference:

Colossians 3:12 (NIV): *"Therefore, as God's chosen people, holy and dearly loved, clothe yourselves with compassion, kindness, humility, gentleness, and patience."*

Here, Paul calls believers to clothe themselves with compassion, reflecting an active and intentional decision to lead with empathy. Leaders in all sectors of ministry and business are called to embody these virtues in their actions and decisions.

Throughout history, inspiring leaders like Nelson Mandela have shown us the incredible power of compassion in guiding leadership. Mandela, who is celebrated for his pivotal role in South Africa's transition away from apartheid, noted, *"There is nothing like returning to a place that remains unchanged to find the ways in which you yourself have altered."* His heartfelt approach allowed him to understand the struggles of his people and work toward mending the relationships between communities separated by racism, hate, and fear.

In today's fast-paced business world, showing compassion is incredibly important. It helps us to take a pause from the hectic pace and gives us a chance to reflect on what truly matters—genuinely supporting our teams and the broader community. This support goes beyond simply using the right words; it involves actively building and nurturing workplaces that promote understanding, value, and appreciation for every individual. When leaders embrace compassion, they enhance their teams' well-being, cultivating an organizational culture filled with collaboration, positivity, and trust.

Compassionate leadership fosters a warm and supportive culture where team members genuinely experience and practice empathy and respect for one another. When leaders show compassion, it promotes loyalty and lifts morale, which often leads to even greater productivity. This environment encourages open communication; employees feel that they can share their thoughts and concerns without fear of judgment. Ultimately, organizations that adopt compassionate leadership enhance employee well-being and create opportunities for greater overall success.

This dynamic is so important— when individuals feel understood and valued, they naturally grow more motivated and dedicated to their roles, boosting their engagement. By placing compassion at the heart of leadership, we open the door to remarkable success. A united and committed team is crucial for reaching our goals and sparking innovation.

Relevance to Business Leaders

For business leaders, compassion may manifest as actively listening to employees' concerns, helping them navigate personal challenges, and demonstrating genuine interest in their well-being. In a business context, this can improve employee retention, foster loyalty, and encourage a collaborative work environment. Leaders who show compassion cultivate stronger relationships and build a more robust workforce, even during economic challenges. Additionally, demonstrating compassion can enhance employee morale, as individuals feel valued and respected within the organization. This positive atmosphere can lead to increased productivity, as employees are more likely to engage in their work when they feel supported. Ultimately, when leaders show compassion, it greatly benefits employees and helps strengthen both their contributions and the overall resilience of the business.

Jesus the Good Shepherd

For the Christian, Jesus is our example of compassionate leadership. His life and ministry perfectly reflect the qualities of profound love, care, and self-sacrifice. His teachings and actions reveal His empathy and commitment to serving others. Jesus' role as the Good Shepherd brings this model of leadership to the forefront, emphasizing the importance of nurturing and guiding those entrusted to our care. This title, Good Shepherd, reflects His steadfast dedication to the well-being of individuals and illustrates that authentic leadership stems from a heartfelt concern for others. By living out these values, Jesus inspires leaders in every field, showing that the measure of successful leadership isn't just authority or power but the depth of compassion and a true dedication to serving others.

As a result, Jesus' approach to leadership has an impact that extends far beyond religious settings; it resonates across various aspects of modern life. Today's leaders in business, education, or community service have a fantastic opportunity to adopt the principles Jesus showcased, helping create spaces filled with empathy and support. By fostering understanding, patience, and selflessness, leaders inspire their teams and communities to unite in pursuit of shared goals, all while nurturing a sense of belonging and purpose. The teachings of Jesus remind us all that genuine leadership isn't just about steering people toward success; it's also about uplifting them through kind acts and service, ultimately creating a more compassionate and connected society for everyone.

Scripture Reference:

John 10:11 (NIV): *"I am the good shepherd. The good shepherd lays down his life for the sheep."*

With these words, Jesus introduces us to the concept of a shepherd's heart—one that is selfless, sacrificial, and dedicated to the welfare of others. Jesus does not simply lead his followers detached and from a distance; He actively engages with them, guiding them closely through trials, protecting them from harm, and offering them the hope of eternal life. His leadership radiates warmth and a heartfelt concern for each person, demonstrating that a leader's true role is to nurture and protect, not just to lead with authority.

This image of the Good Shepherd offers critical insight for modern leaders in all fields. A shepherd knows each of his sheep intimately, and a compassionate leader does the same with their team or congregation. They recognize their team's strengths, challenges, and needs, leading with empathy and insight. A sincere and engaged shepherd never leaves behind one of his own who is struggling; instead, he brings them back into the fold with intentionality and compassion.

Relevance to Church Leaders

Embodying the heart of the Good Shepherd goes beyond simply preaching or teaching. It's about walking alongside people in their struggles, offering guidance in their faith, and being present for them during tough times. When leaders engage actively with their congregation, they create a warm and supportive environment where everyone feels at home.

Moreover, church leaders have a wonderful opportunity to reflect the compassion of Jesus through their actions. By providing pastoral care, spiritual guidance, and unwavering support, they help ensure that each individual feels loved and valued. This heartfelt connection strengthens the community and encourages everyone to grow together in faith.

Leading with Care and Empathy in the Valley

Leadership is often tested during what we call the "valley" moments—those tough times filled with our own challenges, suffering, or predicaments. It's during these periods that compassionate leadership isn't just valuable; it's absolutely essential. A leader who truly understands the struggles of others and shows genuine care during difficult times brings a sense of hope, creating the potential for significant change within their team or community.

During these times, a leader's compassion shines. When leaders genuinely listen to their team, recognize their feelings, and validate their experiences, they foster a sense of trust and safety. This boosts morale and encourages everyone to support one another. Additionally, by sharing a vision of hope, leaders can inspire resilience and motivate their teams to navigate tough times together. Ultimately, these vulnerable moments present a perfect opportunity for leaders to shine and guide their teams through the storm.

Scripture Reference:

Psalm 23:4 (NIV): *"Even though I walk through the darkest valley, I will fear no evil, for you are with me; your rod and your staff, they comfort me."*

In this well-known Psalm, David provided a powerful metaphor for leadership in times of difficulty. Just as a shepherd leads their sheep through dark valleys, so too must a compassionate leader walk with their team through challenges, offering guidance, protection, and comfort. We see in these verses that leadership is not about avoiding hardship but rather navigating it with integrity and care. It's so important to understand that this aspect of leadership truly matters! When leaders embrace compassion, they create a meaningful impact and position themselves to aid transformation in the lives of those who look up to them. This matter holds an immense significance that cannot be overstated.

Relevance to Nonprofit Leaders

In the nonprofit world, leaders often find themselves in challenging environments where resources can be limited, and the communities they serve may face difficult times. Compassionate leadership in this setting is all about being there for others when times are tough. It involves offering emotional and practical support while also keeping a spark of hope alive, even in the face of adversity. A leader's compassion uplifts the team and inspires everyone to keep striving for a brighter future together, making a real difference in the lives of those they serve.

Similarly, business leaders play a crucial role in supporting their teams during challenging times, such as economic downturns, organizational changes, or any crises that may arise. By demonstrating compassion and understanding in these moments, they can foster resilience among employees. This approach encourages everyone to feel more connected to the larger mission, reminding them that they are part of a shared purpose that transcends the difficulties they are currently facing.

Practical Insight: Developing a Shepherd's Heart

Nurturing a shepherd's heart as a leader means taking thoughtful steps to cultivate compassion for ourselves and those around us. It involves dedicating time to accurately understand our team members' needs and perspectives and creating a safe, welcoming environment where everyone feels valued and heard. One effective way to practice empathy is by genuinely listening to your team and responding with kindness and care. By focusing on these connections, we can strengthen our bonds and develop a culture of support and encouragement. While it requires consistent effort and some self-reflection, this is how we can truly embrace the principles of compassion in our daily lives.

Remember, becoming a compassionate leader is not just a one-time goal but an ongoing journey! Authentic leadership centers on relationships and caring for the people around us. By inviting feedback, learning from our experiences, and aligning our actions with our core values, we can continually improve. Establishing habits that demonstrate empathy and under-standing can inspire our colleagues, spreading positivity that elevates the entire team. It may take some time, but with a bit of patience and dedication, you can nurture a shepherd's heart that uplifts and influences others.

66 **Scripture Reference:**

Philippians 2:4 (NIV): *"Let each of you look not only to his own interests but also to the interests of others."*

This scripture encourages believers to develop a mindset that prioritizes others. It tells us to be concerned with the well-being and success of our team members and to be willing to serve. Compassionate leadership requires self-awareness, humil-ity, and a focus on others' needs rather than one's own.

Practical Steps for Leaders

Develop Emotional Intelligence: Emotional intelligence, or EQ, is an important skill! It helps us recognize and manage our own emotions while understanding how others feel. This is key to building healthy relationships, communicating effectively, and handling tricky social situations. When we're in tune with the emotions of those around us, we can respond with empathy and create stronger connections—both at work and in our personal lives. It's crucial for leaders to be attuned to their own feelings and the emotions of their teams. By practicing active listening and demonstrating empathy, they can cultivate a wonderful culture of trust, understanding, and openness. Here are a few more friendly suggestions to help you reach this goal:

- ***Actively Serve Others:*** Jesus set a great example of leadership through service. As leaders, it's essential to show that we're ready to support others, whether that means helping someone out with their work-load or lending a hand during tough decision-making times.

- ***Model Vulnerability:*** Compassionate leaders aren't afraid to show vulnerability. By sharing their own struggles and imperfections, they create a space where everyone feels safe to do the same. This openness builds trust and fosters a warm environment where understanding and compassion can thrive.

- ***Offer Comprehensive Support:*** Compassionate leadership revolves around caring for every aspect of a person, not just their work. It's essential for leaders to look after the mental, emotional, and spiritual well-being of their team. By adopting this approach, we can create a warm and nurturing environment where everyone can thrive together! This fosters a sense of belonging, ensuring that every team member feels valued and understood. Moreover, when leaders demonstrate genuine support for their employees, it enhances overall productivity and job satisfaction. Ultimately, nurturing strong relationships with compassion lays the groundwork for a more resilient and engaged workforce.

Summary

Compassionate leadership is not merely an idea stuck in a textbook; it's a hands-on, transformative approach that can elicit the best in any team! Whether you're leading a business, a church, or a nonprofit, leaders with a shepherd's heart—brimming with compassion, empathy, and care—foster an environment where trust, loyalty, and resilience flourish among their team members.

By following the example of Jesus, the Good Shepherd, leaders can genuinely care for their people and help guide them through the exciting peaks and the tougher valleys that life and work can bring. Compassionate leaders remind us that authentic leadership isn't about power or control; it's all about serving others and making sacrifices when needed. With every little act of compassion, these leaders have the ability to make a big difference in the world!

Application for Business Leaders:

Cultivate deep, empathetic connections with your employees. Commit to your team's emotional and professional development. Be available during challenging moments and provide consistent support. Model exemplary behavior and maintain steady messaging for your team.

Application for Church Leaders:

Embrace servant leadership by prioritizing your congregation's well-being. Provide spiritual guidance and emotional support grounded in biblical principles and sound ethics. Foster a safe environment for vulnerability and shared care.

Application for Nonprofit Leaders:

Demonstrate genuine care for your team and the communities you serve. Promote resilience by spreading compassion, especially during tough times. Create a warm environment of mutual support and shared responsibility. Provide valuable resources and establish networks of service providers eager to collaborate with you in supporting those you serve both within and outside your organization.

Leaders who embrace compassion as a core value will inspire transformative change in their organizations and communities, creating environments where people feel valued and supported. Through their leadership, these leaders will personify the essence of the Good Shepherd and, in doing so, will transform lives for the better.

Chapter 6

Integrity—The Heart Of The Leader

INTEGRITY IS AN ESSENTIAL QUALITY DESIRED IN LEADERS, serving as the cornerstone of effective leadership. In a world filled with scandals that erode our trust—whether in politics, business, or religion—the importance of integrity is more pronounced than ever. Being a leader with integrity means being consistent in your words and actions, standing up for what's right, and adhering to your principles, even when the going gets tough. Integrity is the foundation of effective leadership; without it, building trust and respect is nearly impossible.

Let's explore what integrity looks like in a leadership role and how it comes to life through our actions, and we'll take a look at inspiring biblical figures like Daniel and Joseph, who exemplify integrity. We'll also consider how a decline in integrity among leaders has affected our society and share some practical tips to help build integrity within ourselves and those we lead.

It is imperative for leaders to foster an environment where ethical behavior is prioritized, as this sets the tone for their teams. When we consistently demonstrate integrity, we inspire others to do the same, creating a culture of accountability and trust. Ultimately, integrity enhances individual leadership and also strengthens the overall fabric of society.

The Foundation of Leadership: Integrity

Integrity essentially means being honest and holding strong moral principles. When we think about leadership, integrity becomes the bedrock of all the other qualities a leader should have. A leader's integrity shapes our decision-making, influence over others, and the legacy we leave behind. Without integrity, even the most talented leaders may struggle to gain the trust and respect of their team. In short, integrity is not just a nice-to-have; it's a must-have for any effective leader!

" Scripture Reference:

Proverbs 10:9 (NIV): *"Whoever walks in integrity walks securely, but whoever takes crooked paths will be found out."*

Living with integrity provides us with a sense of security. Leaders who act with integrity do not need to fear being exposed, as actions align with values and principles. Integrity builds trust and enables them to lead confidently, knowing they have nothing to hide. However, those who lack integrity—who "take crooked paths"—will eventually face consequences, as their dishonesty or inconsistency will ultimately be revealed. The story of King David unveils this truth, as the Prophet Nathan conveyed a message from God addressing David's moral failings in his affair with Bathsheba and the murder of her husband. This critical moment is documented in 2 Samuel 12:9-10, *"Why did you despise the word of the Lord by doing what is evil in his eyes? You struck down Uriah the Hittite with the sword and took his wife to be your own. You killed him with the sword of the Ammonites.* ¹⁰ *Now, therefore, the sword will never depart from your house, because you despised me and took the wife of Uriah the Hittite to be your own."*

Integrity in leadership is not about projecting an image of perfection; rather, it emphasizes being consistent, reliable, and truthful. It requires making tough decisions that reflect core values, even when those choices are unpopular or challenging. A leader's integrity significantly influences how words and actions are perceived, fostering a strong culture of trust among followers. This trust is crucial for building a meaningful legacy for any leader. This concept is reinforced by a quote from Former US Senator Alan K. Simpson: *"If you have integrity, nothing else matters. If you lack integrity, nothing else matters."*

Historical Perspective on Integrity

Many inspiring figures in our history have highlighted the significance of integrity in leadership. Abraham Lincoln, the 16th president of the United States, wisely noted, "You can fool some of the people all of the time, and all of the people some of the time, but you cannot fool all of the people all of the time." This famous quote powerfully showcases Lincoln's belief that integrity is the cornerstone of effective leadership and reminds us that when trust is broken, it's often difficult to regain it.

In today's world, leaders like Warren Buffett, the iconic investor, often emphasize the importance of integrity as a key ingredient for long-term success. Buffett once famously said, *"It takes 20 years to build a reputation and five minutes to ruin it."* This is a crucial point about our relationships: trust is fragile and can be easily shaken; therefore, it must be handled with care.

In a world where misunderstandings can occur, nurturing trust requires effort, openness, and commitment. Integrity is central to this journey; it's about holding onto our moral and ethical values while fostering a supportive environment where relationships can flourish. Dedicating ourselves to cultivating integrity isn't just about building trust—it's also about keeping that trust vibrant and alive, highlighting just how essential it is in both our personal and professional lives.

Walking with Consistency in the Valley

Integrity is not only tested during moments of success; it is also proven in the valleys—when a leader faces challenges, dilemmas, or temptation. It is in these moments that consistency of character is essential to navigate difficult situations and emerge with one's integrity intact.

When we think about integrity, it's important to remember that it's not just about avoiding wrongdoing; it's about making the right choice, even when it's difficult. Picture yourself standing at a crossroads where the easy path could lead to short-term gains but might compromise your values. By choosing to adhere to your principles, although the path may present some initial struggles, you will build trust among your team and inspire others to do the same. That is how we become transformational leaders! This ripple effect can cultivate a culture of honesty and accountability, reminding everyone in your sphere of the importance of doing what is right, regardless of the circumstances.

Facing challenges with integrity creates remarkable opportunities for growth. It allows you to learn more about yourself and to demonstrate resilience. Sharing these experiences with others creates a bond of understanding and relatability, fostering an environment where everyone feels supported. It's a reminder that the way we weather life's storms define who we are and strengthens our connections with one another. Embracing this idea can inspire a community that values integrity just as much in adversity as it does during times of great success.

66 **Scripture Reference:**

Psalm 26:1-2 (NIV): *"Vindicate me, Lord, for I have led a blameless life; I have trusted in the Lord and have not faltered. Test me, Lord, and try me, examine my heart and my mind."*

David's heartfelt plea for vindication stems from his strong belief in leading a life of integrity. He's not merely asking for justice; he's inviting God to take a genuine look at his heart and actions. As he reflects on his journey, David underscores that true integrity isn't just a mask we wear during certain moments. Instead, it's a core principle that should resonate in every aspect of our lives. He commits to being authentic, both in public and private, reminding us that integrity is vital for staying true to ourselves.

Leaders often find themselves facing challenges that boil down to critical moments of decision-making, testing their moral values. They must decide between what is easy and right, where the quick fix may seem tempting but could damage their reputation in the long run. From David's perspective, these decisions are not just fleeting moments; they are pivotal points that help shape a leader's legacy. By remaining true to their values, leaders can earn trust and respect, building a legacy that genuinely reflects integrity. This enduring influence emphasizes that the essence of leadership is not solely about doing the right thing when everything is going smoothly, but also about having the courage to make the right choices even when the going gets tough.

Integrity is critical for leaders—it's one of the main building blocks for trust and credibility within a team! Whether times are good or challenging, leaders should adhere to integrity, demonstrating their commitment to ethical choices and principled decisions. Upholding integrity goes beyond personal reputation; it is essential for cultivating a culture of accountability among team members. When leaders exemplify integrity, they inspire their team to follow suit, creating an environment where everyone feels responsible for upholding those values. In essence, a leader's personal integrity produces a ripple effect, influencing team dynamics.

It is important, even though it may feel uncomfortable at times, for leaders to hold team members accountable with the same integrity they exhibit themselves. Approaching accountability with seriousness and sincerity is key—let's avoid any casual attitudes or hidden agendas! This involves fostering clear communication, fairness, and compassion. Everyone on the team should understand how crucial accountability is for achieving our shared goals. Additionally, regularly reviewing these accountability processes is a wise strategy; it allows leaders to assess their effectiveness and make any necessary adjustments. What matters most is maintaining integrity in our relationship with God, just like David, who frequently shared his struggles with Him and openly recognized how much he depended on God to guide his leadership in a manner that honored His Lordship. It's essential to bring any sins or harmful patterns in our lives to the feet of Jesus, as there is simply no other path to a life filled with peace, success, and meaningful impact. By consistently focusing on honesty and relevance in everything we do, leaders can support their teams and create positive outcomes, leading to a more united and high-performing group.

Relevance to Church Leaders

For church leaders, showing integrity means leading by example, especially when faced with tough ethical or moral decisions. During challenging times—whether in our personal lives or at work—church leaders must hold steadfast to their biblical values and seek guidance from God. Whether it's ensuring financial transparency or promoting ethical practices within the community, demonstrating integrity is vital for building and maintaining the trust of our congregations.

Relevance to Nonprofit Leaders

As a nonprofit leader, you may often find yourself in challenging situations with limited resources, which can involve making tough decisions that truly put your integrity to the test. From fundraising to resource allocation and maintaining transparency with donors, it's crucial to stay true to your mission. Embracing integrity in nonprofit leadership entails being committed to the organization's core values and ensuring that every action contributes to the goal of serving the community.

Relevance to Business Leaders

For business leaders, integrity is at the core of all great relationships with employees, customers, and partners. Whether your business is just starting out or has been established for a while, maintaining integrity fosters trust, enhances your reputation, and creates a positive work environment. A business leader who exemplifies integrity is someone who keeps their promises, treats everyone with kindness and respect, and makes ethical decisions, even when no one is watching!

Biblical Examples of Integrity: Daniel and Joseph

Daniel and Joseph, both enslaved and serving foreign kings, truly exemplify integrity and strong values in leadership! Their influence has endured for generations. Take Daniel, for instance, a young Hebrew who became a captive in Babylon. He faced serious challenges that placed him in grave danger, yet he remained true to his faith throughout. His story demonstrates unwavering devotion to God, even during difficult times, as he spent a night in a den with starving lions. This event underscores his bravery and reminds us of how faith and belief can give us strength during tough times that demand courage on our part.

Moreover, Daniel's spiritual gifts, interpreting dreams and visions, showcased his divine wisdom and discernment. This gift not only set him apart from the other "wise men" but also earned him the respect and trust of the Babylonian royalty. His ability to offer deep insights into their dreams made him a valuable member of the royal court, where he positively shaped the direction of the kingdom with honesty and clear morals.

Daniel shows us what a true leader looks like. It's not just about making smart choices or finding success; it's about relying on God and sticking to your spiritual values and principles, even when things get tough. His life is a perfect reminder for all of us to stay true to what we believe in and to lead with courage and conviction.

Similarly, Joseph's story exemplifies resilience and grace in leadership. He endured significant challenges, from being sold into slavery by his own brothers to facing wrongful imprisonment. However, instead of allowing these obstacles to defeat him, they became the backdrop for his remarkable journey.

In Egypt, Joseph's incredible skills and strong character enabled him to rise to important positions—first in Potiphar's house, then in prison, and eventually as a trusted advisor to Pharaoh himself. Like Daniel, one of his standout gifts was interpreting dreams, his favor with others, and playing a crucial role in preventing a national crisis.

Joseph's story serves as a poignant reminder of the importance of wisdom, integrity, and foresight in effective leadership. By interpreting Pharaoh's dream and predicting seven years of plenty followed by seven years of famine, he demonstrated that effective planning truly pays off. His journey reminds us that divine intervention is real and emphasizes God's trustworthy plan for those He has chosen. It shows us that even though what God has called us to may not be easy, with resilience and strong values, we can all navigate tough times. Challenges can become opportunities for greatness, and we can be a guiding light for others facing their own struggles.

These two biblical figures illustrate the importance of personal strength and courage. They serve as a brilliant reminder that authentic leadership involves sticking to our principles, caring for those around us, and inspiring hope and resilience, especially during challenging times.

Scripture Reference:

Daniel 6:4-5 (NIV): *"At this, the administrators and the satraps tried to find grounds for charges against Daniel in his conduct of government affairs, but they were unable to do so. They could find no corruption in him because he was trustworthy and neither corrupt nor negligent."*

Genesis 39:23 (NIV): *"The warden paid no attention to anything under Joseph's care, because* *the Lord was with Joseph and gave him success in whatever he did..."*

Relevance to All Leaders

The stories of Daniel and Joseph offer valuable lessons for all of us. Whether you're at the helm of a business, leading a church, or guiding a nonprofit, embodying the integrity displayed by these remarkable figures can help you earn the trust and respect of those you lead. Their unwavering commitment to strong values, even in tough times, demonstrates how powerful integrity can be in leadership.

Practical Insight: Building Trust Through Integrity

Building trust revolves around integrity. It requires consistent actions, honesty, and a measure of courage to make decisions that genuinely reflect your core values. Keep in mind, trust isn't built in a day; it develops through a series of actions over time that align with your moral compass.

Scripture Reference:

Matthew 5:37 (NIV): *"All you need to say is simply 'Yes' or 'No;' anything beyond this comes from the evil one."*

This verse underscores the importance of honesty and consistency. Leaders who foster trust with their teams, communities, or congregations must be true to their word. Integrity means saying what you mean and doing what you say—there is no room for deception or inconsistency.

Practical Steps for Leaders

1. **Be Transparent:** Leaders must be open and transparent in their actions, especially when mistakes are made. Admitting when you're wrong and correcting course shows integrity and fosters trust.
2. **Follow Through on Commitments:** One of the most important aspects of integrity is keeping promises. Leaders must be reliable and ensure that they follow through on their commitments, regardless of their size.
3. **Lead by Example:** Leaders should model the behavior they expect from others. By demonstrating integrity in every aspect of their work, they inspire others to do the same.
4. **Cultivate Accountability:** Leaders who practice integrity seek accountability for their actions. This includes being open to feedback, taking responsibility, and learning from mistakes.

Summary

Integrity goes beyond being a simple trait—it embodies the essence of leadership. Whether steering a business, a church, or a nonprofit, leaders must nurture integrity as a fundamental value if they wish to foster trust, respect, and long-term success. In today's world, where faith in leadership has been profoundly undermined, the examples set by leaders like Daniel, Joseph, and contemporary figures such as Abraham Lincoln or Warren Buffett underscore the critical importance of integrity.

By consistently embodying integrity, particularly during

challenging times, leaders can foster cultures of trust, loyalty, and respect. These actions will ensure that leaders leave a lasting legacy and transform the organizations and communities they serve.

Application for Business Leaders:

- Keep promises and communicate honestly with employees and customers.
- Make decisions that align with the values of the company, even when it's hard.

Application for Church Leaders:

- Lead by example, showing Christ-like humility, honesty, and transparency in all dealings.
- Maintain a strong moral foundation, making decisions that align with biblical principles.

Application for Nonprofit Leaders:

- Build trust with donors, volunteers, and communities by acting with integrity.
- Ensure the organization's mission is carried out with transparency and accountability.

Leaders who embrace integrity inspire those around them and ultimately leave a legacy that is both impactful and enduring. By consistently demonstrating strong moral principles and ethical behavior, these leaders foster an environment of trust and respect. Their ability to navigate challenges with honesty and transparency not only motivates their team but also sets a standard for others. This commitment to integrity ensures that their influence extends beyond their immediate sphere, creating a lasting impact on future generations and contributing to a culture of accountability and excellence.

Chapter 7

Wisdom—The Crucible Of Discernment

Writer, William Arthur Ward, once said, *"We can learn much from wise words, little from wisecracks, and less from wise guys."* As with most witty sayings, the statement also holds a deeper truth. Wisdom has always been at the heart of great leadership. Although timeless, it's certainly not a relic of the past; in fact, true wisdom is more essential today than ever. It is what helps leaders make decisions that reflect their core values, builds confidence in their teams, and encourages a transformation in all concerned.

Unfortunately, in today's fast-paced world, wisdom sometimes gets pushed aside by short-sighted thinking, quick reactions, and the tendency to choose speed over careful consideration. Let's dive into how wisdom can be integrated into our daily practices, its impact on our legacy, and how a lack of wisdom can affect the efficacy of leadership.

Wisdom is your loyal friend in life's valleys. You know, those moments when everything feels a little wobbly and chaotic? In those times of uncertainty, wisdom arrives like a comforting guide, reminding you that you're never alone. Just picture having wisdom as your closest companion—always eager to share helpful advice, bring clarity, and assist you in navigating through the storms. It's amazing how it brightens our path when we need it the most, transforming those challenging moments into beautiful opportunities for growth and understanding.

The Need for Wisdom in Leadership

Leadership is not just about having that spark of charisma or a set of technical skills. True leadership thrives on godly wisdom to guide us in all significant decisions, especially during those tricky times of uncertainty and chaos (the valley). In those moments when things might seem a bit unclear, great leaders tap into their knack for critically assessing situations and spotting the best paths to take. This understanding goes hand in hand with strong moral integrity and clear thinking. These qualities support leaders themselves and build trust among their teams. When faced with unexpected challenges, wisdom shines like a beacon, lighting the way to safe harbor and ensuring that any decisions reached are made thoughtfully and aligned with shared values and vision.

In today's ever-changing world, leadership thrives on adaptability. Effective leaders, filled with insight, know how to gracefully navigate new situations, using their emotional intelligence to connect with their teams on a personal level. This strong bond fosters trust and motivation, creating a suitable environment where everyone feels valued and inspired to contribute their very best. Essentially, blending emotional intelligence with strategic thinking transforms decision-making into a well-rounded journey that embraces both logical and human elements. The most effective leaders understand this balance, guiding with both their minds and their hearts, ensuring their actions resonate with their followers and nurture a culture of collaboration and excellence.

Scripture Reference:

Proverbs 4:7 (NIV): *"The beginning of wisdom is this: Get wisdom. Though it cost all you have, get understanding."*

Wisdom is often seen as one of the best qualities a leader can have. It's not just about having knowledge; it's about knowing how to use that knowledge to make wise choices in tricky situations. For leaders, the journey toward wisdom is ongoing and involves constant learning, thinking deeply about experiences, and being flexible with new challenges that come their way. This process is important because leaders often encounter challenging moments that require them to handle ethical dilemmas and make decisions that can significantly affect their team and the organization. That's why making wisdom a top priority is essential; it's what helps leaders offer clear guidance and create a supportive atmosphere for everyone.

Wisdom is such a crucial component of leadership; it goes far beyond just aiding in decision-making. It serves as a vital ingredient in shaping a leader's vision and nurturing a strong sense of trust within their team. When leaders embody wisdom, they spot potential challenges and showcase their steadfast commitment to ethical values, which helps to strengthen the confidence of their followers. Trust is the heartbeat of any thriving organization. It's clear how intertwined wisdom, ethical decisions, and trust are – especially for leaders who aspire to foster a strong, successful team and organization. Leaders who act with wisdom are more likely to earn the respect and loyalty of their team members. A wise leader is like a compass, guiding the whole team toward shared success and uplifting outcomes.

Leadership Insight:

Well-known philosopher and physician, Albert Schweitzer, once said, *"Wisdom isn't just something you gather; it's a journey of understanding and living with knowledge."* To lead effectively, it's essential to cultivate and use wisdom—a deep awareness of the values, people, and situations that come into play in leadership. Wisdom, when applied consistently, helps us navigate the everyday challenges and pressures of our roles. It offers us an opportunity to pause and consider the bigger picture and the long-term impacts of our choices. This thoughtful mindset helps us address immediate issues while also paving the way for a brighter future for our teams and organizations. When we welcome wisdom into our roles, we can promote sustainable growth and resilience, guiding our teams and companies towards lasting success.

Relevance to Business Leaders:

For business leaders, wisdom translates into strategic foresight, the ability to navigate market uncertainties, and the discernment to prioritize ethical practices over short-term profits. A wise business leader ensures the organization's sustainability while maintaining integrity.

Relevance to Church Leaders:

Church leaders must embody wisdom to shepherd their congregations effectively, particularly in addressing doctrinal disputes, moral challenges, and community needs. Our ability to discern God's will and apply biblical principles to real-world situations strengthens our ministry's impact.

Relevance to Nonprofit Leaders:

In the nonprofit sector, wisdom guides leaders in allocating resources, engaging stakeholders, and pursuing initiatives that align with their mission. Wise leaders balance passion for their cause with practical discernment, ensuring their organizations serve effectively and ethically.

Solomon's Pursuit of God's Wisdom

King Solomon is often celebrated as a shining example of wise leadership in the Bible. When he had the extraordinary chance to ask God for anything he wanted, Solomon made a truly remarkable choice: he asked for wisdom rather than wealth, power, or even a long life! This choice really shows how he understood just how important wisdom is in leading others. Solomon recognized that being a true leader means having the ability to make good decisions and understand the needs of his people. By choosing wisdom, he was committed to guiding his community with insight and kindness, aiming to serve them better through knowledge and understanding.

" Scripture Reference:

1 Kings 3:9 (NIV): *"So give your servant a discerning heart to govern your people and to distinguish between right and wrong. For who is able to govern this great people of yours?"*

Even in Solomon's request we see what wisdom is all about. It's all about being able to tell right from wrong and making fair decisions, especially when things get complicated. His strong belief in divine wisdom not only shaped how he understood things but also helped shape his remarkable reign filled with prosperity and peace.

Now, let's take a moment to reflect on an important lesson. When Solomon eventually strayed from the wisdom he once embraced, it served as a gentle reminder to all of us about the significance of staying grounded. It's easy to think that those who are wise are infallible, yet even the most enlightened among us can trip up if we close our hearts to relevant guiding principles in Scripture. Staying true to our beliefs can help us navigate life's challenges gracefully and clearly.

Leadership Insight

Billy Graham once remarked, *"The greatest legacy one can pass on to one's children and grandchildren is not money or other material things accumulated in one's life, but rather a legacy of character and faith."* Solomon's early leadership reflects this legacy—a focus on character and divine guidance over personal gain.

Relevance to Today's Leaders

Leaders who seek to embrace Solomon's admirable pursuit of wisdom often cherish the value of humility. They recognize that true wisdom comes from being open to guidance and nurturing a sense of connection to principles bigger than their own understanding. In the business world, this means regularly consulting with mentors, gathering insights from a diverse group of people, and valuing the different perspectives that enhance decision-making. In churches and nonprofits, these thoughtful leaders may take a reflective approach to their decisions, seeking guidance through prayer and engaging in collaborative discussions with their community.

Navigating the Valley with Discernment

As leaders we often find ourselves facing "valley moments." These are challenging times filled with crisis, confusion, or conflict that can really put our skills to the test. During these crucial moments, possessing a sharp sense of discernment and clarity is not just helpful; it's absolutely essential.

Amid uncertainty and pressure, it's vital for leaders to have a steady dose of wisdom guiding us through the challenges we face. Wisdom in this context isn't just about making smart choices; it's about helping us rise above fear and the heavy expectations that might weigh us down. This perspective allows us to make decisions that are not only true to our core values but also genuinely benefit our teams.

By embracing this wisdom, we can provide the guidance and stability our teams crave, particularly in tumultuous times. It fosters an environment of trust and collaboration, helping everyone come together and navigate the stormy seas of uncertainty with confidence and solidarity. In essence, wise leadership can turn difficult moments into opportunities for growth and connection.

Scripture Reference:

James 1:5 (NIV): *"If any of you lacks wisdom, you should ask God, who gives generously to all without finding fault, and it will be given to you."*

James encourages us to seek divine wisdom. When facing uncertainty or difficulty, it's crucial for leaders to turn to spiritual guidance. By taking a moment for prayer, thoughtful reflection and contemplation, we can find the clarity and direction needed to navigate tough situations. This practice is vital and should be embraced by anyone eager to enjoy a long and successful journey in their leadership roles. Embracing this spiritual journey not only enriches our understanding but also empowers us to lead with confidence and compassion.

Leadership Insight

Peter Drucker, the father of modern management, observed, *"Management is doing things right; leadership is doing the right things."* Wisdom helps leaders find the best way forward, even when they have many competing priorities. It ensures that their decisions reflect their mission and values.

Relevance to Business Leaders

Business leaders navigating industry challenges and shifting market dynamics must exercise wisdom by finding the right balance between innovation and long-term stability. It's also important to select the right stakeholders and key team members. By making strategic and thoughtful decisions—assessing risks and choosing individuals who truly resonate with the company's vision—leaders play a vital role in fostering growth and building a lasting future success.

Relevance to Church Leaders

For church leaders, navigating the valley often involves addressing sensitive issues such as moral failures, doctrinal disagreements, or societal challenges. Wise leaders tackle these situations with kindness, a touch of humility, and a positive focus on making things better.

Relevance to Nonprofit Leaders

Nonprofit leaders often navigate resource-limited environments where wisdom is essential for prioritizing initiatives, making strategic decisions, and responding effectively to crises. Discernment enables them to maximize their impact, steward resources responsibly, and stay aligned with their mission, values, and the needs of the communities they serve.

Practical Insight: Seeking God's Wisdom Amid Uncertainty

Wisdom isn't something we're born with; it's a quality we grow and develop over time. It comes from experiences that challenge our perspectives and encourage us to think deeply about our choices and their impact. Honest self-reflection helps us recognize how even the smallest decisions shape our lives and those around us. For many, turning to God adds an even richer dimension to this journey, offering moral guidance and clarity when faced with complexity. Proverbs 9:10 reinforces this idea, reminding leaders in church, business, and nonprofit sectors that true wisdom begins with a deep reverence for God. In leadership, decisions carry weight, affecting people, organizations, and communities. When leaders anchor their choices in the fear of the Lord, they gain wisdom that goes beyond strategy—it is rooted in integrity, humility, and a higher purpose. Understanding comes from knowing God, equipping leaders to navigate challenges with discernment, steward their responsibilities well, and inspire those they serve with vision and righteousness.

Leaders who make the journey of wisdom are in a fantastic position to tackle the challenges of their roles. By focusing on thoughtful decision-making, we can boost our own skills and set an example for everyone around us. As leaders we can nurture trust and confidence within our teams when our actions show we genuinely care about the well-being of others. During tough times, wisdom serves as a warm companion, shining a light to help us find our way through uncertainty with ease. It encourages leaders to make choices that meet immediate goals and nurture strong relationships and a culture of integrity. So, this commitment to wisdom isn't just about personal growth; it's about creating a supportive environment where trust and collaboration can thrive, paving the way for lasting success.

Scripture Reference:

Proverbs 2:6 (NIV): *"For the Lord gives wisdom; from his mouth come knowledge and understanding."*

This verse reminds us just how important it is to seek this precious gift through heartfelt prayer, scripture study, and the wise counsel of those who live by God's principles. When leaders ground their decisions in God's wisdom, they enrich their judgment and also strengthen their capacity to navigate the challenges and uncertainties that life presents. So, let's come together and sincerely embrace this important call to seek wisdom.

Practical Steps for Cultivating Wisdom

1. **Prayer and Reflection**: Make it a habit to seek God's guidance through prayer, and spend some time reflecting on scripture, especially the book of Proverbs. This practice helps connect leaders with divine principles and brings clarity to your journey!

2. **Lifelong Learning:** Keep learning and growing by reading, seeking mentorship, and connecting with different viewpoints. Great leaders are always open to new experiences and ideas.

3. **Cultivate Empathy:** Wisdom is all about understanding what others need and how they feel. When leaders show empathy, their decisions not only connect with their followers but also create a supportive and encouraging environment.

4. **Practice Patience:** Wisdom takes a bit of patience. It resists the "tyranny of the urgent"— that impulsive urge to react and allowing yourself the time to thoroughly consider everything.

Leadership Insight

Mahatma Gandhi once remarked, *"It is unwise to be too sure of one's own wisdom. It is healthy to be reminded that the strongest might weaken and the wisest might err."* This insight highlights the importance of humility, a key trait for effective and thoughtful leadership. When leaders embrace humility, they open themselves to ongoing growth and learning. Recognizing that even the mightiest among us can face challenges and that everyone, no matter how wise, can make mistakes helps leaders stay grounded and relatable. In a world where confidence can sometimes drift into arrogance, this quote gently nudges us toward self-reflection and understanding. By acknowledging our limitations, we can create a nurturing environment that encourages open dialogue, collaboration, and shared learning, ultimately leading to more thoughtful and compassionate decision-making. So, let's treasure the gift of wisdom and aspire to a leadership style that values humility, growth, and the beauty of lifelong learning!

Application for Business Leaders:

- Approach decisions with both strategic foresight and ethical consideration.
- Build teams that value collaboration and diverse perspectives.

Application for Church Leaders:

- Model humility and discernment in addressing moral and spiritual challenges.
- Seek God's guidance to navigate complex congregational needs.

Application for Nonprofit Leaders:

- Prioritize initiatives that align with the organization's mission and values.
- Foster transparency and accountability to build trust with stakeholders.

Summary

Wisdom has always been an essential ingredient in effective leadership, even as our society's values and priorities rapidly change over time. In a world that often values speed and efficiency, the importance of wisdom shines through. It's not just about having knowledge; it's about making thoughtful decisions built on a blend of experience, insight, and personal values. Leaders who embrace wisdom create a workplace where decisions are made thoughtfully rather than impulsively. This deeper understanding helps us tackle challenges with confidence and encourages others to do likewise.

Leaders who value this principle earn the trust and respect of their teams, vital for long-term success. By focusing on lasting impacts instead of quick wins, we set the stage for meaningful transformation within our organizations and communities. Visionary leaders are true change agents, inspiring innovations that are effective, ethically responsible, and socially aware. Their legacy of wisdom, rooted in trust and respect, establishes a strong foundation for leadership that adapts to today's challenges while preparing for future opportunities. Together, they are making a meaningful difference that goes far beyond individual accomplishments.

Taking the time to nurture wisdom puts us in an excellent position to inspire confidence in our teams and stakeholders and foster an environment where growth and innovation can thrive! This confidence creates a strong and lasting foundation for authentic, positive changes in our organizations and communities. By demonstrating wisdom, we establish a solid groundwork for building a lasting legacy. This legacy is closely tied to our ability to make thoughtful choices and remain focused on our purpose. In turn, we provide a meaningful way to guide future generations, sharing values that promote success, ethical choices, and a commitment to the greater good.

Chapter 8

Faithfulness—Steady In The Storm

"The true mark of a leader is the willingness to stick with a bold course of action... even as the rest of the world wonders why you're not marching in step with the status quo." — Bill Taylor

FAITHFULNESS IS ALL ABOUT STICKING TO YOUR CAUSE, purpose, or calling, even when challenges, distractions, and temptations come knocking. In the world of leadership, being faithful is a reflection of a leader's character and can be a comfort and anchor during uncertain times. It is unfortunately quite common to come across leaders who seem focused on personal gain, quick wins, or fleeting successes which leads to the sad neglect of faithfulness in their leadership.

Faithfulness isn't just a nice quality; it's a fundamental part of being an effective and enduring leader. It keeps us grounded in our core values and principles, helping to build trust and integrity. When we embrace faithfulness, we will naturally build a strong foundation for our credibility, inspiring those around us to pursue long-term goals rather than just seeking temporary successes. In the end, this commitment ensures a positive impact that goes beyond immediate rewards, allowing us to create a meaningful legacy that resonates with our teams and stakeholders.

The Power of Faithfulness in Leadership

Being faithful is at the heart of building confidence in leadership. When we think about effective leaders, a few key virtues stand out. Steadfastness— it means consistently doing what you say you will do, which helps create a solid foundation of trust between you and your team. Accountability means you step up and take responsibility for your actions and decisions, which strengthens the trust between you and your followers. And let's not forget about... Commitment— showing dedication to the success and well-being of your team, demonstrating empathy and offering support every step of the way. When we bring all these elements together, it creates a sense of organizational momentum and stability that paves the way for success!

Leaders who embody these qualities create an environment where individuals feel secure and valued. By demonstrating faithfulness to their values and to those they lead, such leaders inspire confidence in their capabilities. This kind of confidence builds strong loyalty among team members, creating a close-knit and motivated group. When followers trust their leader's integrity and commitment, they're much more likely to dive into their tasks with enthusiasm and share in the leader's vision, which leads to mutual success.

" **Scripture Reference:**

Proverbs 20:6 (NIV): *"Many claim to have unfailing love, but a faithful person who can find?"*

How rare and precious is faithfulness in our relationships? For leaders, being faithful is exceedingly important because it helps build trust and creates lasting bonds with employees, congregants, and stakeholders alike.

Leadership Insight

Teacher and biblical scholar Oswald Chambers observed, *"It is inbred in us that we have to do exceptional things for God, but we have to be exceptional in the ordinary things."* Grounded leaders grasp this idea; they realize it's the small, everyday actions that matter the most, not just the grand, showy gestures. Those little things, done consistently, create a real impact!

Relevance to Business Leaders

Being faithful in businesses means sticking to good ethical practices, providing top-notch quality for customers, and being there for employees when times get tough. This approach not only builds a loyal customer base but also keeps the team motivated and happy!

Relevance to Church Leaders

For church leaders, being faithful is all about staying true to God's Word, nurturing your congregations like a loving shepherd, and facing challenges with unwavering dedication. It's about growing together as a community and supporting each other in faith, whether times are good or tough.

Relevance to Nonprofit Leaders

In the nonprofit world, faithfulness shows up as a heartfelt commitment to push through challenges, keeping the organization's mission front and center, and making sure to stay accountable to your generous donors and constituents. It's all about staying dedicated, no matter the odds!

Faithfulness in the Valley: A Leader's Endurance

At the heart of leadership is faithfulness, a vital quality that helps us find our way through tough times—you know, those times filled with challenges, crises, or uncertainty. Faithfulness builds a solid sense of integrity, keeping us true to our values even when the going gets tough. This strong commitment doesn't just help us stay strong, it also motivates our team! By showing faithfulness, we embody resilience, making it an essential trait for great leadership and decision-making when things become a bit rocky.

Scripture Reference:

Galatians 6:9 (NIV): *"Let us not become weary in doing good, for at the proper time we will reap a harvest if we do not give up."*

In other words, stay strong and trust that your hard work will pay off in time. Being faithful during tough times shows resilience and can inspire others to keep going right alongside you.

Leadership Insight

Martin Luther King Jr. once said, *"The ultimate measure of a man is not where he stands in moments of comfort and convenience, but where he stands at times of challenge and controversy."* Faithful leaders stand firm and resolute during tough times, displaying endurance that inspires their followers. By facing challenges with unwavering strength, we model the importance of persistence and hope, reminding everyone that together, we can overcome any adversity. Our steadfastness becomes a type of guidance that brings a sense of comfort and motivation to those who look up to us.

I wholeheartedly agree with King's statement. I remember the inspiring leaders in my life who never backed down when faced with tough times. Some of them showed incredible courage, pressing on even when the odds were stacked against them. One in particular who comes to mind is my uncle, a man of unshakable faith who pioneered a small church in the heart of New York City's Lower East Side during the late 1950s—a time when crime and addiction gripped the streets. Despite the dangers surrounding him, he pressed forward, believing that light could pierce even the darkest places. Week after week, he preached hope to the hopeless, prayed with struggling families, and opened the church doors to anyone in need. Over the years, his steadfast dedication transformed the church into a thriving community of believers, where former addicts found redemption, children grew up with strong faith, and passionate leaders emerged to carry the vision forward. When he eventually relocated with his family to Connecticut, he left behind more than just a building—he left a legacy of love, faith, and a church that stood as a beacon of God's unwavering presence in the neighborhood. That church community still exists there to this day.

Beyond the great heroes of faith, I've been fortunate to witness the strength of godly men and women who embodied these qualities right before me. Their influence didn't stop there; many of those leaders have encouraged me over the years to remain strong and resolute, even when giving up felt like the easier choice. Their unwavering faithfulness and determination inspire me every day. I truly feel blessed!

Relevance to Business Leaders:

Leadership challenges, such as team capitulation, interpersonal conflicts, and fierce market competition, can test the determination of business leaders. But those who effectively navigate these challenging times while staying true to their values often become stronger and more resilient!

Relevance to Church Leaders:

Church leaders face a variety of challenges—spiritual, relational, and financial—but their unwavering faith allows them to persevere. Their commitment not only strengthens their own spiritual resilience but also acts as a source of stability and hope for those they lead. In times of adversity, their steadfast trust in God's guidance inspires others to stay faithful, creating a ripple effect that bolsters the entire community.

Relevance to Nonprofit Leaders:

Nonprofit leaders often navigate unpredictable landscapes,

facing challenges such as funding shortages, political obstacles, and shifting community needs. Their commitment to their mission keeps them motivated, driving their efforts and instilling confidence in their supporters.

The Parable of the Talents and Faithful Servants

Jesus' parable of the talents illustrates what it means to be good stewards and leaders. It reminds us that by tending to our smaller tasks, we're paving the way for exciting new opportunities. Just think of it like planting little seeds; with some love and attention, they can flourish into something much bigger and more rewarding. When we embrace this mindset, it can lead to incredible benefits not just for ourselves but for everyone around us, fostering a wonderful community filled with hope and progress.

Scripture Reference:

Matthew 25:21 (NIV): *"His master replied, 'Well done, good and faithful servant! You have been faithful with a few things; I will put you in charge of many things. Come and share your master's happiness!'"*

The master celebrates the servant's unwavering faithfulness, emphasizing how his dedication has led to greater trust and future responsibility. It serves as a wonderful reminder that when we are diligent and faithful in our current roles, we build credibility and prepare ourselves for an even greater impact in the future. By managing our responsibilities effectively, we pave the way for new opportunities and challenges. Trustworthiness and hard work yield benefits in the long run.

Leadership Insight

Max DePree, a renowned leadership expert, wrote, *"The first responsibility of a leader is to define reality. The last is to say thank you. In between, the leader is a servant."* When we explore faithfulness in the realm of servant leadership, we uncover a quality that makes a true difference. A faithful servant leader embraces their responsibilities with heartfelt dedication and genuine care. They don't simply check off tasks; they are wholeheartedly committed to serving others, ensuring that every job is approached thoughtfully and with sincere intentions. By being reliable and diligent, they inspire trust within their team, nurturing a positive atmosphere where everyone is lifted to higher ground. In the end, faithfulness in this role is all about building lasting relationships and celebrating success together!

Relevance to Today's Leaders:

- **Business Leaders:** Faithful stewardship of resources, employees, and customers builds a solid foundation for growth and success.
- **Church Leaders:** Faithfulness in ministry ensures the spiritual and relational health of the congregation.
- **Nonprofit Leaders:** Faithful management of donor funds and program initiatives strengthens trust and impact.

Practical Insight: Staying Committed to Your Mission

Faithfulness is an active commitment that flourishes through intentionality and discipline. When we wholeheartedly dedicate ourselves to our mission—especially in the face of distractions or setbacks—we can skillfully navigate challenges and uplift those around us. This unwavering dedication extends beyond immediate goals. Ultimately, the leaders who embrace this level of commitment leave a meaningful legacy that resonates with future generations, creating a ripple effect of positivity and purpose that can transform lives.

Several leaders come to mind when I think about faithfulness, and one of them is Pastor David Wilkerson. He wholeheartedly followed God's calling, establishing Times Square Church in October 1987. The church initially gathered in Town Hall before eventually moving to its permanent home at the Mark Hellinger Theater, where his ministry continued to impact countless lives. As the founding pastor, he preached powerful biblical messages that emphasized righteous living and unwavering dependence on God. His commitment to discipleship and leadership development also led him to establish the Summit International School of Ministry in 1994, which serves as the Bible school of Times Square Church. Decades earlier, in 1958, he founded Teen Challenge, a ministry dedicated to helping individuals overcome addiction through Christ-centered recovery. Later, in 1971, he launched World Challenge, an organization committed to global evangelism and humanitarian aid. His passion for raising leaders, discipling believers, and serving the poor remains at the core of Times Square Church's mission today.

Another remarkable example of a leader who demonstrated unwavering faithfulness is Charles Swindoll. As a pastor, author, and educator, he has devoted his life with laser-like focus to teaching biblical truths with clarity and compassion. In 1979, he founded *Insight for Living*, a radio broadcast ministry that has reached millions worldwide with practical, Christ-centered messages. Swindoll also served as the president and later chancellor of Dallas Theological Seminary, where he helped equip future generations of Christian leaders. Through his decades of ministry, he has written numerous books, pastored thriving churches, and remained steadfast in his mission to encourage believers to walk faithfully with God. His leadership has left a lasting impact on countless lives, demonstrating the power of faithfulness in ministry.

How can you take a moment today to honor the leaders in your network who led with faithful hearts and determination, leaving a lasting impact on your life?

Scripture Reference:

2 Timothy 4:7 (NIV): *"I have fought the good fight, I have finished the race, I have kept the faith."*

The apostle Paul's words serve as a profound reminder to all leaders about the importance of staying faithful until the very end of their journey. Being committed to your mission means embracing perseverance, keeping your focus, and nurturing a lasting sense of purpose. Let's aim to finish strong together.

> *"Being faithful in the smallest things is the way to gain, maintain, and demonstrate the strength needed to accomplish something great."*

> — Alex Harris

Practical Steps for Cultivating Faithfulness

1. **Clarify Your Mission:** Clearly define your purpose and values as a leader. This clarity serves as an anchor during challenging times.

2. **Prioritize Relationships:** Faithfulness is relational. Invest in meaningful connections with employees, congregants, or stakeholders.
3. **Practice Accountability:** Regularly evaluate your actions and decisions against your stated values and goals.
4. **Seek Support:** Connect with mentors, advisors, and friends who nurture loyalty and offer support!

Leadership Insight

The historian Arnold Toynbee observed, "History is a vision of God's creation on the move." Leaders who remain true to their values and principles make a significant difference in the narratives of their organizations and communities. They create a legacy that extends beyond their immediate environment, positively influencing future generations. Their commitment can inspire others and foster confidence that nurtures a supportive atmosphere filled with perseverance and integrity. This means their impact lasts long after they are gone. When leaders are consistent in their actions and decisions, they are not only making a difference today; they are also paving the way for a brighter tomorrow. This is how leaders create a lasting impact and legacy.

Summary

Faithfulness is a trait that enhances the effectiveness of leadership. Unfortunately, it often gets overlooked in today's fast-paced world. Staying committed to our core principles can sometimes feel challenging due to the constant rush for quick results and instant gratification. We can observe the impact of this lack of faithfulness in various ways, from public scandals exposing moral lapses to corporate greed prioritizing profits over people. Such actions can significantly undermine trust and indicate a troubling trend of making decisions without careful consideration. When we forget to remain true to our values, we risk damaging our credibility, which can ultimately affect the entire organization we strive to support.

On the other hand, if we remain faithful and steadfast, embracing authenticity, we will contribute to a culture of integrity and perseverance within our teams. By adhering to our values, mission, and commitment to our followers, we foster an environment where individuals feel motivated, inspired, and genuinely invested in a shared vision. By building long-lasting relationships founded on trust and accountability, we foster loyalty not only to ourselves but to the broader vision of the organization. Being faithful is a crucial element of strong leadership, helping to restore public trust in leaders everywhere. It shows that integrity and steadfastness are key components for achieving lasting success.

Application for Business Leaders:

- Uphold ethical practices and long-term commitments, even in competitive or challenging markets.
- Foster a culture of loyalty and accountability within your organization.

Application for Church Leaders:

- Model faithfulness in personal character, spiritual leadership, and pastoral care.
- Encourage your congregation to persevere in their faith journeys.

. . .

Application for Nonprofit Leaders:

- Demonstrate consistency in pursuing your organization's mission despite limited resources or obstacles.
- Build trust by maintaining transparency and accountability with donors and beneficiaries.

Faithful leaders serve as beacons of stability, inspiring trust, and resilience in those they lead. By cultivating faithfulness, leaders can navigate the storms of governance and create a heritage of enduring impact and purpose.

Chapter 9

Teamwork – The Power Of Community

Teamwork plays a vital role in the success of organizations. It involves individuals coming together, sharing their unique skills and perspectives to achieve common goals. Fostering effective teamwork enhances each person's strengths, creating a vibrant and innovative environment where fresh ideas can flourish. It builds trust and promotes open communication, both of which are essential for nurturing a supportive organizational culture. Sometimes, we overlook just how important teamwork is and how it requires intentionality and a selfless attitude. With that in mind, let's take a moment to consider the benefits of collaborating as we explore several monumental examples of teamwork:

1. **The Beatles** – Individually, the members of this world-famous band were gifted and capable musicians and songwriters. However, their mastery and the extent of their talent were best showcased when each of the four members came together to form this anomaly of a band. As a result of their

cooperation and teamwork, they transformed the music landscape for an entire generation.

2. **Apple Computer** – This company stands out as one of the most transformational brands in the world of technology! Founded in 1976 by the visionary Steve Jobs and his brilliant partner Steve Wozniak, this small start-up has impacted lives worldwide. Although both men may have achieved individual success, together they created something extraordinary—not only technology but also a culture and lifestyle that millions still enjoy today.

3. **Jesus and His Twelve Disciples** – The significance of teamwork and collaboration truly shines through in Jesus's ministry and his remarkable group of followers—his inner circle. Even though Jesus had the power to accomplish everything by Himself, He thoughtfully and lovingly included these men in a movement that has touched billions of lives, transformed nations, and created a lasting legacy of hope.

Teamwork and collaboration are shown in the example set by Jesus himself. The insights we glean from leaders worldwide illustrate this important truth. It's evident that coming together, whether in smooth sailing or during tough times, creates a meaningful impact that makes everything worthwhile.

It's the wonderful combination of teamwork and community spirit that truly strengthens organizations, enabling them not only to survive but thrive. In challenging moments, it's heartening to witness how the collective resilience and adaptability of a team can help an organization withstand adversity. Together, they can emerge even stronger on the other side, demonstrating that collaboration and support make all the difference. Let's celebrate these unforgettable moments of unity! Each individual plays a vital role in achieving our shared goals, which makes our collective journey genuinely uplifting.

Throughout my journey in business and nonprofit leadership, I've discovered that teamwork truly lies at the heart of every meaningful win and accomplishment. Early on, I realized that "no one is an island onto themselves" and that success is rarely a solo endeavor. This notion resonates clearly in a well-known quote by the renowned athlete Michael Jordan: "*Talent wins games, but teamwork and intelligence win championships.*" It reminds us that while individual talent plays a vital role in reaching our goals, it's our collaboration and shared thoughts that drive us toward remarkable success together. This reality becomes most evident in the difficult times spent in the valley.

As we explore the current leadership landscape, it's clear that technology, social media, and personal ambitions have captured the attention of our culture. Today's business trends showcased on social media have romanticized the idea of solopreneurs and independent success stories. However, we know that most successful outcomes stem from collaboration and partnerships. Therefore, we must recognize the vital role of leaders who foster a culture of cooperation and demonstrate their dedication to shared values, inclusivity, and teamwork. They understand that embracing collaboration leads to outstanding results for their organizations and nurtures valuable experiences and growth for team members. This supportive environment creates a strong sense of belonging and purpose, which is essential in today's business world.

The Strength of Leading Together

Leadership thrives when we work together as a team. Great leaders understand that their achievements aren't just their own; they are built on the amazing talents and contributions of everyone on their team. In fact, the combined strength of a close-knit team can often outshine any one leader. By creating a supportive atmosphere that values collaboration, we can help our teams to brainstorm new ideas, tackle challenges creatively, and assist one another along the way. This teamwork boosts productivity and creates a culture of respect and shared dreams.

Scripture Reference:

Ecclesiastes 4:9-10 (NIV): *"Two are better than one, because they have a good return for their labor: If either of them falls down, one can help the other up. But pity anyone who falls and has no one to help them up."*

The writer, whom many believe to be Solomon, highlights the importance of mutual support and collaborative effort in any environment. When leaders embrace teamwork, they cultivate a positive atmosphere where individuals feel valued and supported. It's all about creating a community where everyone can thrive together, fostering a sense of belonging that encourages each person to contribute their best. Emphasizing teamwork can lead to amazing outcomes, as people become motivated and engaged when they know they have each other's backs.

Leadership Insight

John C. Maxwell wrote, *"Teamwork makes the dream work, but a vision becomes a nightmare when the leader has a big dream and a bad team."* Effective leaders invest in building strong teams, recognizing that their success depends on the collective effort of their team.

Relevance to Business Leaders:

Teamwork enables business leaders to pool limited resources, delegate effectively, and foster innovation. Collaborative leadership encourages employees to take ownership of their roles, creating a culture of accountability and shared success.

Relevance to Church Leaders:

Church leaders rely on teamwork to fulfill their mission. By involving congregants and staff in ministry efforts, they build a stronger community that reflects the unity of Christ.

Relevance to Nonprofit Leaders:

Nonprofits depend on volunteers, donors, and staff working in harmony. A leader's ability to foster teamwork ensures the effective delivery of services and the organization's sustainability. This is another strong selling point that draws in donors and funding sources.

Biblical Principles of Teamwork: The Body of Christ

The Bible provides a compelling framework for teamwork through the metaphor of the body of Christ. Each member has a unique role, yet all are interdependent.

66 Scripture Reference:

1 Corinthians 12:12-14 (NIV): *"Just as a body, though one, has many parts, but all its many parts form one body, so it is with Christ. For we were all baptized by one Spirit so as to form one body... Now if the foot should say, 'Because I am not a hand, I do not belong to the body,' it would not for that reason stop being part of the body."*

These familiar verses underscore the importance of both diversity and unity in achieving a successful team. When team members come from different backgrounds, experiences, and perspectives, they can share unique ideas and solutions that enrich the team. By recognizing diversity, we are positioned to celebrate it, knowing that every individual's contribution is valued and matters. By appreciating and integrating our team's unique strengths, we create a welcoming and collaborative environment where everyone feels valued and empowered. This environment fosters teamwork and promotes innovation, leading to improved problem-solving and achieving shared goals.

Leadership Insight

Mother Teresa once remarked, *"I can do things you cannot, you can do things I cannot; together we can do great things."* Leaders who embrace this perspective cultivate a culture where everyone's contributions are respected and celebrated. We must rely on one another – we can see from history that our success and notable achievements depend on collaboration.

Relevance to Today's Leaders

- **Business Leaders:** Encouraging collaboration between departments or individuals with different skills enhances innovation and efficiency.
- **Church Leaders:** Empowering members to serve strengthens the church's mission.
- **Nonprofit Leaders:** By harnessing the unique talents of each team member and volunteer, we create a dynamic and engaging environment that ensures that our collective efforts have a broader impact.

Building a Cohesive Team in the Valley

Challenging times can put a team's strength and togetherness to the test! In the midst of these valleys it's extremely important for leaders to create a warm environment where everyone feels united, safe, and resilient. This doesn't just mean keeping spirits high; it's also about encouraging teamwork, open communication, and offering a great deal of support. When leaders help everyone feel like they belong and share a common goal, they can tackle difficulties together more efficiently, turning challenges into opportunities for growth and bonding within the team.

Scripture Reference:

Exodus 17:12 (NIV): *"When Moses' hands grew tired, they took a stone and put it under him and he sat on it. Aaron and Hur held his hands up—one on one side, one on the other—so that his hands remained steady till sunset."*

This story illustrates the remarkable power of teamwork in supporting leaders, especially during challenging times when they may feel vulnerable. It's truly inspiring to see how effective leaders motivate and nurture strong teams that unite like a close-knit family, uplifting one another in times of need. When this occurs, success becomes something the entire team can share. It doesn't belong to just a few, but to everyone.

When challenges arise, having a united team is like possessing a secret weapon. They can offer the encouragement and strength that leaders often times require to navigate tough situations. Together, they cultivate an environment where everyone feels valued and empowered, transforming obstacles into incredible opportunities for personal and collective growth and success. These are the moments when team members who typically stay in the background often rise to the occasion, providing a talent, idea, or support that propels the team across the finish line. Teamwork during times of crisis or high-pressure situations brings many heroes out of hiding. So, let's celebrate the magic of teamwork and the remarkable moments it creates.

Leadership Insight

Former U.S. President Harry S. Truman said, *"It is amazing what you can accomplish if you do not care who gets the credit."* Leaders who genuinely care about their team's unity—more than just pursuing personal accolades—create a wonderful environment where collaboration can thrive. When leaders prioritize the needs of the team over their own success, they nurture strong bonds among team members, making it easier for everyone to work together harmoniously and support one another. In such a supportive atmosphere, ideas can flow freely, innovation is stimulated, and everyone feels motivated to contribute. It's a win-win situation for both the team and the organization.

Relevance to Leaders

- **Business Leaders:** Organizational crises, interpersonal conflicts, and operational disruptions provide opportunities for team members to collaborate creatively and devise effective workflow and process solutions.
- **Church Leaders:** During spiritual or community crises, teamwork ensures that the church remains a sanctuary of refuge and hope, preventing anyone from falling through the cracks.
- **Nonprofit Leaders:** When facing financial or operational challenges, a close-knit team can make all the difference in keeping the mission on track, ensuring funders are satisfied, and meeting community needs.

Practical Insight: Empowering Others Through Collaborative Leadership

Empowering others is at the heart of collaborative leadership! It's all about sharing responsibilities, putting your trust in team members, and working together to create a sense of ownership. Research shows that teams with empowered members are 60% more engaged and produce better innovative solutions, which underscores the effectiveness of collaborative leadership in driving success.

Scripture Reference:

Proverbs 27:17 (NIV): *"As iron sharpens iron, so one person sharpens another."*

This verse highlights how important it is to work together. Real and meaningful growth happens when people come together selflessly to achieve a common goal. Leaders who focus on empowering their team members play a crucial role in this process. By creating a warm environment where everyone feels appreciated and motivated to pitch in, we help build a culture of continuous partnership and cooperation. This boosts everyone's skills and makes sure that success is celebrated by all, fostering a sense of community and teamwork. In simple terms, the magic that happens through teamwork and empowerment helps people grow and propels the organization forward as a cohesive unit.

Practical Steps for Cultivating Teamwork

1. **Communicate Vision Clearly:** Share your vision and goals openly, ensuring everyone understands their role in achieving them.
2. **Celebrate Diversity:** Recognize the unique strengths, experiences, and perspectives of each team member.
3. **Encourage Collaboration:** Provide opportunities for team members to work together on projects and initiatives.
4. **Foster Trust:** Build an environment where team members feel safe to share ideas and take risks.
5. **Provide Resources and Support:** Equip your

team with the tools and training they need to succeed.

Leadership Insight

Ken Blanchard, the brilliant mind behind *The One Minute Manager,* reminds us, *"None of us is as smart as all of us."* When leaders embrace this truth, they unlock the unhindered potential of their teams. It's like finding a treasure chest over-flowing with talent, creativity, and innovation just waiting to be discovered. By nurturing a warm environment that values trust, collaboration, and open communication, leaders can truly inspire their team members to shine their brightest.

Relevance to Today's Leaders

- **Business Leaders:** Delegating authority and trusting employees boosts morale, creativity, and productivity.
- **Church Leaders:** Empowering lay leaders enhances ministry impact and nurtures future leaders.
- **Nonprofit Leaders:** Encouraging collaboration among stakeholders strengthens advocacy efforts and service delivery.

Summary

Teamwork is a vital part of outstanding leadership, showcasing a leader's commitment to shared values and the success of the whole team. In our fast-paced, often individualistic world—where technology can sometimes make us feel alone—collaboration is more important than ever. Leaders who encourage team-work show that they truly appreciate every member's input and are dedicated to building an open and friendly environment for sharing ideas. This spirit of collaboration empowers everyone on the team, making them feel proud of their roles and inspiring them to work together towards a common goal, which ultimately boosts creativity and productivity.

Working together as a team to tackle today's challenges is crucial. When we set transformative goals—whether it's changing how our organization works, achieving project success, or making a difference in our community—we really need the diverse experiences and skills that come from a collaborative effort. Leaders who embrace teamwork spark trust and loyalty in their teams and boost problem-solving by bringing out the best in everyone. By fostering a friendly, team-focused environment, we help our organization succeed and create a sense of shared purpose that allows both leaders and team members to shine in their pursuits.

Application for Leaders

- **Business Leaders:** Foster a collaborative workplace culture where employees feel valued and motivated.
- **Church Leaders:** Model the unity of the body of Christ by involving diverse members in ministry efforts.
- **Nonprofit Leaders:** Build strong partnerships and collaborative networks to amplify impact.

When leaders promote teamwork, they build a legacy that goes far beyond what they can achieve alone. Just like the

Apostle Paul said, *"From him the whole body, joined and held together by every supporting ligament, grows and builds itself up in love, as each part does its work"* (Ephesians 4:16, NIV). By harnessing the strength of community, these leaders achieve their goals and inspire others to participate in the journey.

Chapter 10

The Return To The Mountain—
Reflections And New Horizons

In the realm of leadership, "The Return to the Mountain" symbolizes a significant adventure that leaders are urged to undertake for authentic growth and maturity. Envision this journey as a profound reflection where individuals can face their challenges and glean valuable lessons from the difficulties they've encountered. Overcoming these obstacles goes beyond personal accomplishment; it's about broadening your vision and uncovering your true purpose. By immersing yourself in this transformative experience, you will gain clarity and insights crucial for navigating the complexities of leadership. This journey equips you with a renewed sense of purpose, preparing you to motivate others and cultivate a culture of innovation and resilience.

The idea of "The Return to the Mountain" is important for leaders in many spheres, whether in businesses, churches, or nonprofit organizations. Each of these areas has its own set of challenges that can sometimes feel a bit daunting. By embracing the lessons learned from the journey, leaders in these fields can build a solid foundation based on empathy, community, and teamwork. When we grasp the meaning behind this metaphor, we can put its principles into action, tackling the challenges at hand as well as paving the way for a lasting impact. By taking in the wisdom from our own experiences, we create a culture that encourages learning, promotes growth, and ultimately sets the stage for sustainable success for our organizations.

The Journey from the Valley to the Summit

The journey from the valley to the summit is a wonderful metaphor for how we grow and change over time, full of ups and downs that shape our paths. In this story, the valleys stand for the tough times and challenges that every leader faces. But as we have learned, these struggles are also fantastic opportunities for learning and growth. They push us to dig deep, confront our fears and weaknesses, and think about how we can improve. Every challenge we encounter in the valley is a wonderful opportunity to develop our resilience through self-reflection. This process helps us acquire the essential skills and insights we'll need to scale the mountain ahead. It's often in these tough moments that the foundations of great leadership take shape, allowing us to bounce back stronger and more capable than we were before.

> *"If there is not the war, you don't get the general; if there is not a great occasion, you don't get a great states-man; if Lincoln had lived in a time of peace, no one would have known his name."*
>
> — Theodore Roosevelt

On the flip side, summits represent those incredible moments of success and achievement that come after working hard through the valleys. Reaching the summit isn't just about celebrating success; it's also a time for us to pause and take in the bigger picture of our vision and purpose. At this high point, true leaders reflect on their journeys, appreciate the challenges they've overcome, and strengthen their commitment to ongoing growth. Valleys and summits are deeply connected, reminding us that leadership isn't just about winning; it's also about the resilience we show during challenging times. This relationship creates transformative leaders who are not only empathetic and insightful but are also eager to help others navigate their own unique journeys.

Scripture Reference:

James 1:2-4 (NIV): *"Consider it pure joy, my brothers and sisters, whenever you face trials of many kinds, because you know that the testing of your faith produces perseverance. Let perseverance finish its work so that you may be mature and complete, not lacking anything."*

James' words emphasize how embracing challenges can be seen as a golden opportunity for growth and maturity. It's a wonderful reminder that every obstacle we face can help us climb up from the valley of our struggles to the summit of our achievements. These experiences help shape us into the wonderful individuals God intends us to be for His glory. Every moment is meaningful to God; they all play a vital role in His beautiful master plan for our lives. By tackling these challenges head-on, we can develop resilience and gain valuable insights that propel us forward on our journey. In short, the valley and the mountain work hand in hand in the process of development and refinement. So, let's welcome those challenges with open arms, knowing they are stepping stones toward our personal and professional development.

Leadership Insight

Theodore Roosevelt observed, *"It is hard to fail, but it is worse never to have tried to succeed."* Leadership involves embracing challenges and understanding that adversity is often a stepping stone to growth. When we confront risks with optimism, our vision becomes clearer, much like the bright peak of a mountain that stands tall against the backdrop of the valley's trials. Ultimately, these experiences in the valley not only strengthen our resolve but also pave the way for insightful and effective leadership.

Relevance to Leaders

- **Business Leaders:** Navigating competitive markets, unengaged teams, and financial instability encourages leaders to think strategically, adapt with resilience, and create a culture of innovation and accountability that truly inspires everyone involved.
- **Church Leaders:** Tackling spiritual crises, limited volunteer engagement, and community issues enhances faith and mission.
- **Nonprofit Leaders:** Overcoming negative media or community perceptions, funding and operational hurdles builds credibility and effectiveness.

Leading with Renewed Strength and Vision

Returning to the summit gives leaders a wonderful sense of accomplishment, along with a refreshing and broader view of their roles and the challenges ahead. This moment isn't just about celebrating past successes; it's also a great opportunity for us to reflect on our journeys and experiences, discovering valuable insights that can help shape future strategies. Plus, it's such a wonderful opportunity to imagine new possibilities and explore creative ways to help your organization thrive—let's keep those dreams flowing!

By connecting these aspirations to your organization's core values, you can ensure your vision is both ambitious and deeply rooted in the principles that define your mission and culture. This alignment fosters a sense of unity that inspires and motivates teams to come together and work towards shared goals, ultimately leading to stronger momentum and greater outcomes.

Scripture Reference:

Habakkuk 3:19 (NIV): *"The Sovereign Lord is my strength; he makes my feet like the feet of a deer, he enables me to tread on the heights."*

Habakkuk highlights the concept of divine empowerment, illustrating how it aids us in overcoming difficulties. It underscores the significance of this empowerment in achieving greater success. Ultimately, this theme is crucial for renewing leadership and inspiring growth.

Leadership Insight

"The greatest danger in times of turbulence is not the turbu-

lence itself, but to act with yesterday's logic." – Peter Drucker. Leaders who journey through challenging times and rise back to the summit do so with fresh perspectives, becoming guides who inspire others to chase common dreams together. Let's embrace the valuable lessons from yesterday without staying stuck in the past. Focusing solely on what's behind us can be risky. As leaders, we have the exciting opportunity to learn from our experiences while keeping our eyes set on the future for ourselves and our teams.

Relevance to Leaders

- **Business Leaders:** A refreshed perspective allows for innovative strategies and market adaptability.
- **Church Leaders:** Renewed vision fosters spiritual growth and community engagement. It keeps us engaged with what God is doing "now."
- **Nonprofit Leaders:** Clear goals and consistent energy enable teams to tackle pressing social issues with a renewed perspective and determination.

Scripture Reference:

Isaiah 40:31 (NIV): *"But those who hope in the Lord will renew their strength. They will soar on wings like eagles; they will run and not grow weary, they will walk and not be faint."*

Here, Isaiah describes us as people on a heartfelt journey powered by faith and strength, leading to amazing accomplishments and a meaningful impact. His words highlight the spiritual refreshment that uplifts us during difficult moments, encouraging believers to tackle challenges with steadfast courage.

Leadership Insight

Dietrich Bonhoeffer wrote, *"Action springs not from thought, but from a readiness for responsibility."* Leaders who find strength in their faith usually feel well-equipped to handle their responsibilities and embrace those around them who want to lend their support. The leader's beliefs empower the team with the courage to tackle challenges with a positive spirit, helping to inspire individuals to chase their own dreams with enthusiasm and dedication.

Relevance to Leaders

- **Business Leaders:** Belief in a greater purpose and strength fosters resilience and creativity amid significant economic uncertainties.
- **Church Leaders:** Faith-centered leadership inspires congregations and aligns ministry efforts with God's will.
- **Nonprofit Leaders:** Trusting in divine guidance helps leaders to stay motivated as they passionately advocate for the needs of community members.

Practical Insight: Embracing New Challenges with Purpose and Clarity

Climbing back up the mountain isn't just about reaching the top; it's about starting a thrilling new adventure filled with fresh opportunities and possibilities. Each climb brings its own unique challenges, reminding us that growth often comes from facing tough situations. For leaders aiming for these heights, it's important to see this journey as more than a finish line—it's an invitation to grow and evolve. It is a perfect time to look back at what we've learned from past experiences and use those insights to tackle new tasks ahead. This positive mindset turns challenges into exciting opportunities for innovation and growth, helping us build a stronger connection with the journey and our ultimate goals.

In this ever-changing world, leaders have a special role, guiding our teams through uncertain times. By creating a space filled with purpose and clarity, we empower our teams to face new challenges head-on with confidence and determination. Each challenge we meet teaches us resilience and adaptability, making our leadership journey all the richer. It's so important for us to appreciate the value of our experiences and to intentionally incorporate those lessons into our strategies. This way, every step we take can guide us toward a bright and exciting new future! In other words, let's not take anything for granted. Instead, let's look for lessons in every challenge and every success. There's so much to learn, and by sharing what we discover, we can inspire those we lead!

Practical Steps for Leaders

1. **Reflect and Recalibrate:** Periodically assess past decisions and lessons learned to refine future strategies for yourself and those you lead.
2. **Recast Vision:** Reaffirm organizational values and align them with evolving goals and challenges. Values fuel the engine of your organization.
3. **Cultivate Collaboration:** Cultivate a culture of trust, inclusion, and shared purpose to empower teams. This unity can enhance your vision.

4. **Commit to Lifelong Growth:** Stay curious and embrace ongoing learning to adapt in our ever-changing world. It takes purpose and determination to grow together!

5. **Stay Anchored in Faith:** Make it a practice to regularly seek divine guidance to help keep your actions and decisions in harmony with spiritual principles. Remember, without faith, it will be challenging to please God and fulfill His beautiful plan for your life.

Leadership Insight

Peter Drucker said, *"The best way to predict the future is to create it."* Proactive leaders who accept change can make a meaningful impact and position themselves to leave a lasting legacy. This legacy inspires others and withstands difficult seasons and the test of time.

Summary

"The Return to the Mountain" means embarking on an exciting journey that goes beyond task management—it's at the core of transformative leadership. This journey is all about committing to your personal and professional growth, staying renewed, and looking ahead with a positive mindset. As leaders embark on this adventure, they create an environment that motivates their teams to think outside the box and confidently tackle challenges. Charles Swindoll once said, *"In life's valleys, we often find ourselves trapped by doubts. However, true leaders rise above these valleys through faith and perseverance. Each step they take inspires others—not just with words, but through their unwavering spirit to overcome obstacles."* These remarkable leaders not only lift their teams but also foster a culture of resilience and innovation, which is so important in today's fast-paced world.

The lasting impact of effective leadership is closely linked to the leaders who wholeheartedly embrace the "Return to the Mountain" philosophy, prioritizing their mission and vision, and choosing to focus on lasting success over immediate gains. They understand that authentic leadership isn't just about personal wins but about the growth and success of the people they lead. As Leadership expert Simon Sinek puts it, *"Leadership is not about being in charge. Leadership is about taking care of those in your charge."* By living out the principles of transformative leadership, these leaders make sure their influence lasts, inspiring future generations to overcome their own valleys and reach for greater heights and influence.

Scriptural Encouragement:

Philippians 3:13-14 (NIV): *"Brothers and sisters, I do not consider myself yet to have taken hold of it. But one thing I do: Forgetting what is behind and straining toward what is ahead, I press on toward the goal to win the prize for which God has called me heavenward in Christ Jesus."*

Here we are encouraged to embrace a forward and upward-focused mindset. It highlights the importance of continually striving for growth and achievement, reminding us that the journey of leadership is one of evolution and self-discovery. By fostering a culture of innovation and positivity, leaders can inspire their teams to reach new heights, celebrate each milestone, and recognize that every step forward contributes to a brighter future. Let's keep pushing boundaries together.

Final Application

- **Business Leaders:** Innovate and adapt with resilience, fostering sustainable growth.
- **Church Leaders:** Lead with faith and a renewed sense of mission that inspires spiritual transformation.
- **Nonprofit Leaders:** Tackle challenges with clarity and purpose, driving meaningful collective impact.

By actively engaging and embracing continuous learning, we gain a richer understanding of how we influence others, creating a sense of accountability within our own teams. This positive ripple effect inspires team members to embark on their own growth journeys, resulting in increased motivation and productivity throughout the organization. When we equip our successors with these essential skills and values, they help ensure that the organization's vision remains alive, nurturing resilience and adaptability for whatever the future brings.

Chapter 11

Living The Leadership Journey

The concept of "Living the Leadership Journey" is pivotal in understanding that leadership is not about achieving a singular goal but rather involves a rich tapestry of experiences that shape our character and purpose. This journey is characterized by ongoing development and adaptation, where we face a series of challenges that test our resolve and commitment. Each experience—whether a triumph or a setback—contributes to our development, reinforcing the idea that leadership is not fixed but is dynamic and multifaceted.

It's important to highlight how focusing on values during tough times makes all the difference. In those challenging times, we truly see what leadership is all about. When leaders stick to their values, they not only find their own way through the storm but also encourage their teams to do the same. This dedication to principles builds trust and loyalty, which is the cornerstone of a leader's legacy. As leaders look back on their experiences, it's evident that the toughest challenges often lead to the strongest bonds and leave a lasting impression on those they guide, creating a story that goes well beyond personal accomplishments. A wonderful example of this truth can be found in the inspiring life and ministry of Dr. Tim Keller. Throughout his journey, he shared many meaningful lessons, such as the significance of blending intellectual diligence with deep faith, placing the needs of others before personal ambitions, and the incredible power of interpreting the Gospel while staying true to its essence. His life was punctuated by his legacy as a dedicated leader, an engaging teacher, and a true lover of God's Word. Though he may be gone, his incredible work lives on through the many lives he touched and the wonderful ministries he built.

The Journey Up the Mountain

Think of leadership as a long-lasting trek up a mountain - every step is both a challenge and an opportunity! As we climb higher, we encounter various hurdles that test our resolve and resilience. From making tough choices to navigating team dynamics, these challenges push us to adapt and grow. Every obstacle we conquer expands our skillset and deepens our understanding of ourselves and our teams. This part of the journey is crucial; it encourages us to step beyond our comfort zones, embrace our vulnerabilities, and enhance our emotional intelligence. The lessons learned from these experiences create a strong foundation for whatever awaits us.

Being a leader is a lot like going on an adventure! It's not just about reaching the mountain peaks; it's also about finding our way through the valleys that come along the path. These valleys can represent challenging times, such as uncertainty, setbacks, or moments of disappointment. During these times, it's completely normal for leaders to feel overwhelmed, wondering if they have what it takes or if they're guiding their teams in the right direction. But guess what? It's often in these valleys that we experience amazing growth! We learn to embrace humility, seek feedback, and build strong partnerships with our team members. As we navigate these challenging times, we frequently discover renewed strength and a clearer sense of purpose. Ultimately, the journey of climbing mountains and wandering through valleys adds richness to a leader's experience. It creates a beautiful tapestry of skills and insights that make us more effective and compassionate guides for others.

Scripture Reference:

Ecclesiastes 3:1 (NIV): *"There is a time for everything and a season for every activity under the heavens."*

This verse is a sobering reminder for all leaders about the ups and downs of life and their important roles. It encourages us to fully embrace every season we face. By doing this, we will act with purpose and keep going, no matter what our journey brings —whether we find ourselves in a valley or climbing to a summit.

Leadership Insight

Former U.S. President Dwight D. Eisenhower remarked, *"Leadership is the art of getting someone else to do something you want done because he wants to do it."* Effective leaders recognize that their influence grows through these cycles, as they learn to adapt and inspire.

Embracing the Fullness of the Leadership Experience

Starting on the adventure of leadership is an exciting journey filled with ups and downs that we must embrace with open arms. It's important to tackle this path with humility, knowing that every challenge is a chance to learn and grow. Let's not forget the power of gratitude; it helps us recognize the incredible support from our teams and the valuable lessons we gain from our successes and hurdles. A strong commitment to both personal and professional growth is key, as it keeps us evolving and adjusting to our ever-changing world. In the end, the beauty of being a leader lies in the variety of challenges and victories we face, all of which contribute to shaping who we are and how effective we can be.

" **Scripture Reference:**

Philippians 4:12-13 (NIV): *"I know what it is to be in need, and I know what it is to have plenty. I have learned the secret of being content in any and every situation, whether well fed or hungry, whether living in plenty or in want. I can do all this through him who gives me strength."*

Paul's words inspire us to find contentment in our journeys. He highlights how crucial it is to harness our inner strength to overcome challenges, encouraging us to embrace every moment with gratitude and a down-to-earth outlook. This uplifting message truly resonates at every step of the leader's journey, reminding us all that a healthy perspective can make a significant difference in our lives. It's a wonderful reminder that we should always take a moment to celebrate the little victories and stay grateful for the silver linings we find in each situation. Everyone deserves to feel hopeful, and this message embodies that spirit perfectly!

Leadership Insight

Howard Schultz, former CEO of Starbucks, noted, *"When you're surrounded by people who share a passionate commitment around a common purpose, anything is possible."* The leadership journey is enriched by shared experiences and collective growth. It also helps carry teams and individuals through the inevitable periods of testing in the valley.

Relevance to Leaders

- **Business Leaders:** Building a culture of collaboration and shared vision fosters resilience and hope.
- **Church Leaders:** Embracing a wide range of ministry experiences deepens spiritual impact and expands the scope of vision.
- **Nonprofit Leaders:** Valuing and understanding both successes and setbacks enhances organizational adaptability.

Leading Others to New Heights

Leadership is more than just advancing yourself; it's about taking on the rewarding responsibility of helping others find and unleash their incredible potential! A true leader doesn't just focus on their own journey to the top; instead, they shine as a friendly beacon of encouragement for everyone around them, guiding them to discover their own paths—especially in tough times, which can feel like navigating a vessel through quicksand. This beautiful journey of lifting others up requires a mix of essential qualities: a clear vision that makes the path clear and inspires; empathy that helps leaders understand the dreams and challenges of their team; and a servant's heart that emphasizes the importance of putting others first, creating a space where growth and teamwork can truly thrive. Ultimately, great leadership is all about building a strong community where everyone can rise together, supporting each other as they reach for new heights and achieve amazing things side by side.

Scripture Reference:

Matthew 20:26-28 (NIV): *"Whoever wants to become great among you must be your servant, and whoever wants to be first must be your slave—just as the Son of Man did not come to be served, but to serve, and to give his life as a ransom for many."*

Christ modeled servant-leadership, emphasizing the significance of serving others while leading. His life showcases the values of humility and selflessness in leadership roles.

Leadership Insight

True leadership lifts those around us, sparking a wonderful ripple of growth and achievement. Bill Bradley beautifully captured this sentiment when he stated, *"Leadership is unlocking people's potential to become better."*

Relevance to Leaders

- **Business Leaders:** Empowering employees cultivates innovation and loyalty.
- **Church Leaders:** Guiding congregations to spiritual maturity fulfills the church's mission.

- **Nonprofit Leaders:** Mentoring team members strengthens organizational capacity.

Leadership Beyond the Summit

Reaching the summit is just the beginning of an incredible journey! It's an invitation for leaders to use their influence in exciting ways to create a lasting impact in their communities and beyond. Authentic leadership goes beyond personal goals and success; it's all about building a meaningful legacy filled with integrity, fresh ideas, and support for others. This type of leadership not only inspires today but also creates a reliable foundation for future generations, fostering an environment where kindness, responsibility, and creative thinking can truly thrive. By lifting those around us, we, as leaders, can transform our communities and contribute to a vibrant culture of positive change that lasts long after we pass the baton.

Scripture Reference:

2 Timothy 4:7 (NIV): *"I have fought the good fight, I have finished the race, I have kept the faith."*

Paul's reflection serves as a potent reminder for leaders. It emphasizes the importance of perseverance in our journey. Additionally, it urges us to stay true to our calling and mission to the very end.

Leadership Insight

Martin Luther King Jr. once said, *"The ultimate measure of a man is not where he stands in moments of comfort and conve-*

nience, but where he stands at times of challenge and controversy." Effective leadership extends beyond mere achievement; it is significantly tested by one's capacity to inspire others. Integrity and resolve are crucial qualities in this process, setting a strong example for those around us. Ultimately, a leader's true measure is not just in their own success but in their ability to elevate and motivate others toward a shared vision.

Relevance to Leaders

- **Business Leaders:** Creating a legacy of ethical practices ensures long-term success.
- **Church Leaders:** Building a spiritually vibrant community leaves a lasting impact.
- **Nonprofit Leaders:** Establishing sustainable programs and initiatives fosters enduring change.

Practical Application: Living the Leadership Journey

1. **Commit to Lifelong Learning:** Stay curious and open to new ideas, continuously expanding your knowledge and perspective.
2. **Build a Support Network:** Surround yourself with mentors, peers, and team members who share your vision and values.
3. **Practice Reflection:** Regularly evaluate your decisions to ensure they align with your values and goals.
4. **Invest in Others:** Prioritize the growth and development of those you lead.
5. **Stay Grounded in Faith:** Seek spiritual

guidance to navigate challenges with wisdom and grace.

Leadership Insight

Brene Brown said, *"What we know matters, but who we are matters more."* Embracing the leadership journey is all about showcasing the principles that truly reflect your character and values. A life that's truly fulfilling shines through in the way we demonstrate those core values in every moment of each day.

Leadership is an exciting journey filled with challenges and valuable lessons, especially during those inevitable tough "valley seasons" that test our resolve. In these ten chapters, we've explored how, as leaders, we can shine in moments of triumph and when facing adversity. It's during these challenging times that we need to stay strong, showcasing resilience and a heartfelt commitment to our vision and values.

A big theme we've discussed is transformation and empowerment. I encourage you to see obstacles as stepping stones rather than roadblocks. This mindset shift is significant, as it empowers us to tackle challenges while inspiring others to join us on the journey. Leadership is all about driving change; it's about taking personal challenges and turning them into opportunities for the whole team. Together, we can make significant strides forward.

We should also remember that leadership isn't a solo endeavor! Each chapter highlighted the importance of teamwork and collaboration, showing how engaging others in our journey is key to overcoming difficulties. Inspiring leaders uplift their teams, fostering an atmosphere where everyone feels empowered to contribute, especially during tough times. It's a win-win for everyone involved: both the leader and the team.

As we've walked through these chapters, I've attempted to

underscore the importance of self-reflection and ongoing growth. Great leaders make it a priority to look back on their experiences, learning valuable lessons from both their triumphs and their stumbles. This practice sharpens our abilities but also equips us to support others during tough times, showing that resilience is a vital quality in successful leadership. It's essential to strike a balance in this process, as we certainly don't want to dwell on past wins or losses. Let's reflect, learn from our experiences, and keep moving forward together.

Leading through those challenging moments calls for a positive mindset, a focus on empowering others, and a commitment to shared progress. By nurturing these traits, we can motivate our teams and turn obstacles into stepping stones for growth. At its heart, the leadership journey is about lifting each other up and ensuring that, even during tough times, we come out stronger together.

Living the leadership experience is more than just personal achievements; it's also about fostering collective growth and making a positive impact. As leaders, let's aim to leave the world a bit better than we found it through our mindful actions. This journey is truly meaningful, with every step contributing to a larger purpose and ensuring that our efforts resonate beyond our immediate circles.

As you navigate life's ups and downs, remember to always strive for new heights. Embrace the learning moments and growth opportunities that come your way; every challenge is a stepping stone that helps you build resilience and wisdom, two key ingredients for effective leadership. Stay dedicated, and don't just lift yourself up—help lift those around you too.

I hope this book has inspired you to appreciate both the climb to success and the experiences we gain in the valleys. You can't have one without the other; they go hand in hand in this adventure called life. By embracing this idea, you're setting yourself up for personal growth while also empowering others to shine. Remember, the bumps you hit in the valley seasons aren't forever; they're simply opportunities for learning and development. Each step you take through adversity makes you stronger and prepares you for amazing heights ahead!

As you navigate your highs and lows, I encourage you to continue seeking new lessons and embracing your growth. Don't hesitate to welcome the discomfort of the valleys, as they often bring the richest rewards. I'd love to hear your stories from these valleys and the insights you've gained along the way. Let's celebrate the wonderful journey of growth and the amazing transformations that arise from embracing all of life's ups and downs. You and your team will flourish as a result of the inevitable return to the valley.

> *"The marvelous richness of human experience would lose something of rewarding joy if there were no limitations to overcome. The hilltop hour would not be half so wonderful if there were no dark valleys to traverse."*
>
> — Helen Keller

Keep climbing. Keep growing!

Leadership Reflections

LEADERSHIP ISN'T JUST A POINT YOU REACH; INSTEAD, IT'S A wonderful and ongoing journey filled with growth, learning, and the joy of service. In light of this, I invite you to engage in reflection activities to enhance your voyage. These activities are designed to help deepen your leadership skills and understanding, make a meaningful impact, and inspire your team members to join you on this exciting adventure.

This section has been thoughtfully designed with you in mind, aiming to enrich your experience as you further explore the chapters you've just read. Each brief reflection introduces important leadership principles intertwined with biblical wisdom and practical insights from the chapters. Through engaging scripture verses, reflective questions, and uplifting quotes, this process invites you to take a closer look at yourself, ultimately advancing your growth as a leader. I look forward to walking alongside you on this exciting path of development.

Chapter 1: The Leader's Calling — More Than a Mountain

- **Focus**: Understanding the divine and personal call to leadership.
- **Key Scripture**: *"For I know the plans I have for you," declares the Lord, "plans to prosper you and not to harm you, plans to give you hope and a future."* (Jeremiah 29:11)
- **Leadership Quote**: *"He who has hope has everything."* - St. Augustine

Reflection Questions:

1. What experiences in your life have affirmed your calling to leadership?
2. How does your leadership role align with your purpose and values?

Activity: Write a personal mission statement that reflects your leadership calling.

Chapter 2: Humility — The Soil of Spiritual Leadership

- **Focus**: Cultivating humility as the foundation of effective leadership.
- **Key Scripture**: *"Humble yourselves before the Lord, and he will lift you up."* (James 4:10)
- **Leadership Quote**: *"Pride makes us artificial and humility makes us real."* — Thomas Merton

119

Reflection Questions:

1. In what ways can humility strengthen your leadership?
2. How do you handle feedback or criticism in your leadership journey?

Activity: Identify three areas where humility can improve your effectiveness as a leader.

Chapter 3: Perseverance — The Valley of Strength

- **Focus**: Developing resilience to endure challenges and setbacks.
- **Key Scripture**: *"Let us not become weary in doing good, for at the proper time we will reap a harvest if we do not give up."* (Galatians 6:9)
- **Leadership Quote**: *"It always seems impossible until it's done."* — Nelson Mandela

Reflection Questions:

1. What challenges have shaped your leadership resilience?
2. How can you inspire perseverance in your team during difficult times?

Activity: Create a plan for overcoming a current or anticipated challenge in your leadership role.

Chapter 4: Vision – The Eyes of Faith in the Valley

- **Focus**: Crafting and casting a compelling vision.
- **Key Scripture**: *"Where there is no vision, the people perish."* (Proverbs 29:18)
- **Leadership Quote**: *"Leadership is the capacity to translate vision into reality."* — Warren Bennis

Reflection Questions:

1. How does your vision inspire others?
2. What steps can you take to align your team with your vision?

Activity: Develop a vision statement for a project or initiative you are leading.

Chapter 5: Leading with Compassion – The Shepherd's Heart

- **Focus**: Building trust and fostering empathy in leadership.
- **Key Scripture**: *"Be shepherds of God's flock that is under your care, watching over them."* (1 Peter 5:2)
- **Leadership Quote**: *"People don't care how much you know until they know how much you care."* — Theodore Roosevelt

Reflection Questions:

1. How do you demonstrate compassion in your leadership?
2. What actions can you take to better understand the needs of your team?

Activity: Write down three ways you can show compassion to your team this week.

Chapter 6: Integrity — The Heart of the Leader

- **Focus**: Upholding integrity in all aspects of leadership.
- **Key Scripture**: *"The integrity of the upright guides them, but the unfaithful are destroyed by their duplicity."* (Proverbs 11:3)
- **Leadership Quote**: *"Integrity is doing the right thing, even when no one is watching."* — C.S. Lewis

Reflection Questions:

1. What does integrity mean to you as a leader?
2. How do you ensure your actions align with your values?

Activity: Identify a decision where integrity was or will be critical. Reflect on how you approached or will approach it.

Chapter 7: Wisdom – The Crucible of Discernment

- **Focus**: Applying wisdom to make sound decisions.
- **Key Scripture**: *"If any of you lacks wisdom, you should ask God, who gives generously to all without finding fault, and it will be given to you."* (James 1:5)
- **Leadership Quote**: *"Wisdom is not a product of schooling but of the lifelong attempt to acquire it."* — Albert Einstein

Reflection Questions:

1. How do you seek wisdom in your decision-making process?
2. What role does discernment play in your leadership?

Activity: List three recent decisions you've made. Reflect on how wisdom influenced those decisions.

Chapter 8: Faithfulness – Steady in the Storm

- **Focus**: Remaining committed and reliable in all circumstances.
- **Key Scripture**: *"Well done, good and faithful servant!"* (Matthew 25:23)
- **Leadership Quote**: *"Faithfulness in the small things leads to faithfulness in the big things."* — Hudson Taylor

Reflection Questions:

1. How do you remain faithful to your responsibilities during challenging times?
2. What does faithfulness look like in your daily leadership?

Activity: Identify one area where you can demonstrate greater faithfulness and create a plan to act on it.

Chapter 9: Teamwork – The Power of Community

- **Focus**: Harnessing the strength of collaboration.
- **Key Scripture**: *"Two are better than one, because they have a good return for their labor."* (Ecclesiastes 4:9)
- **Leadership Quote**: *"If you want to go fast, go alone. If you want to go far, go together."* — African Proverb

Reflection Questions:

1. How do you foster collaboration within your team?
2. What steps can you take to build a stronger sense of community?

Activity: Develop a plan to enhance collaboration and communication within your team.

Chapter 10: The Return to the Mountain — Reflections and New Horizons

- **Focus**: Reflecting on growth and preparing for the next phase of leadership.
- **Key Scripture**: *"Forgetting what is behind and straining toward what is ahead, I press on toward the goal to win the prize for which God has called me heavenward in Christ Jesus."* (Philippians 3:13-14)
- **Leadership Quote**: *"Life can only be understood backwards; but it must be lived forwards."* — Søren Kierkegaard

Reflection Questions:

1. What have you learned from your leadership journey so far?
2. How will you apply these lessons to future challenges?

Activity: Write a reflection on how you have grown as a leader and identify one goal for your future development.

Scripture To Consider In the Valley

Blessed is the man who remains steadfast under trial, for
when he has stood the test he will receive the crown
of life, which God has promised to those who
love him.

— James 1:12 ESV

Not only that, but we rejoice in our sufferings,
knowing that suffering produces endurance, and
endurance produces character, and character
produces hope, and hope does not put us to shame,
because God's love has been poured into our
hearts through the Holy Spirit who has been given
to us.

— Romans 5:3-5 ESV

I can do all things through him who strengthens me.

— Philippians 4:13 ESV

Count it all joy, my brothers, when you meet trials of
various kinds, for you know that the testing of your
faith produces steadfastness. And let steadfastness
have its full effect, that you may be perfect and
complete, lacking in nothing.

— James 1:2-4 ESV

But he said to me, "My grace is sufficient for you, for my
power is made perfect in weakness." Therefore I will
boast all the more gladly of my weaknesses, so that
the power of Christ may rest upon me. For the sake of
Christ, then, I am content with weaknesses, insults,
hardships, persecutions, and calamities. For when I
am weak, then I am strong.

— 2 Corinthians 12:9-10 ESV

Come to me, all who labor and are heavy laden, and I
will give you rest.

— Matthew 11:28 ESV

Have I not commanded you? Be strong and courageous.
Do not be frightened, and do not be dismayed, for the
Lord your God is with you wherever you go."

— Joshua 1:9 ESV

If we endure, we will also reign with him; if we deny
him, he also will deny us;

— 2 Timothy 2:12 ESV

"Come, let us return to the Lord; for he has torn us, that
he may heal us; he has struck us down, and he will
bind us up.

— Hosea 6:1 ESV

Because you have kept my word about patient
endurance, I will keep you from the hour of trial that
is coming on the whole world, to try those who dwell
on the earth.

— Revelation 3:10 ESV

Strengthening the souls of the disciples, encouraging
them to continue in the faith, and saying that through
many tribulations we must enter the kingdom
of God.

— Acts 14:22 ESV

Who comforts us in all our affliction, so that we may be
able to comfort those who are in any affliction, with
the comfort with which we ourselves are comforted
by God.

— 2 Corinthians 1:4 ESV

If the God of my father, the God of Abraham and the Fear of Isaac, had not been on my side, surely now you would have sent me away empty-handed. God saw my affliction and the labor of my hands and rebuked you last night."

— Genesis 31:42 ESV

For affliction does not come from the dust, nor does trouble sprout from the ground,

— Job 5:6 ESV

So we do not lose heart. Though our outer self is wasting away, our inner self is being renewed day by day. For this light momentary affliction is preparing for us an eternal weight of glory beyond all comparison, as we look not to the things that are seen but to the things that are unseen. For the things that are seen are transient, but the things that are unseen are eternal.

— 2 Corinthians 4:16-18

Many are the afflictions of the righteous, but the Lord delivers him out of them all.

— Psalm 34:19 ESV

Let no one say when he is tempted, "I am being tempted by God," for God cannot be tempted with evil, and he himself tempts no one. But each person is tempted when he is lured and enticed by his own desire. Then

desire when it has conceived gives birth to sin, and
sin when it is fully grown brings forth death.

— James 1:13-15 ESV

For my sighing comes instead of my bread, and my groan-
ings are poured out like water.

— Job 3:24 ESV

For whatever was written in former days was written for
our instruction, that through endurance and through
the encouragement of the Scriptures we might have
hope.

— Romans 15:4 ESV

Fear not, for I am with you; be not dismayed, for I am
your God; I will strengthen you, I will help you, I
will uphold you with my righteous right hand.

— Isaiah 41:10 ESV

If you faint in the day of adversity, your strength is small.

— Proverbs 24:10 ESV

It is good for me that I was afflicted, that I might learn
your statutes.

— Psalm 119:71 ESV

Scripture To Consider In the Valley

Rejoice in hope, be patient in tribulation, be constant in prayer.

— Romans 12:12 ESV

About the Author

John Rivera is the founder of Vive Consulting. He is a dynamic thought leader, mentor, and voracious reader—a dedicated student of all things leadership. He is also the author of "The Climb: Practical Lessons for Today's Leader." John has over two decades of senior-level experience in effective process management and team leadership. He excels at leading major projects from start to finish! His passion for mentoring both emerging and experienced leaders truly stands out. In this role, he fully commits to discovering and nurturing skills and talents that enhance performance and ensure everything operates at an exceptional level.

John comes from vibrant New York City, where he was raised in a loving Christian household. His journey with the Lord began at a young age, and by the time he turned seventeen, he was already involved in ministry, sparking a lifelong passion that continues to inspire him every day.

This remarkable leadership journey began in youth ministry during the 1980s, and his passion for serving leaders has only grown stronger since then. Over the years, he has embraced various leadership roles in the local church, including deacon, teacher, ministry leader, and overseer—each filled with purpose and dedication. In the early 1990s, John started honing his skills as a trainer and consultant, concentrating on organizational and leadership development. Through this role, he has joyfully supported numerous churches and nonprofit organizations, assisting them in growing, finding clarity in their vision, and achieving excellence in everything they do.

In the 2000s, John assumed the role of Director of Ministry Relations at a New York City radio station. He passionately supported churches throughout the tri-state area with his valuable expertise, helping them enhance their outreach and ministry efforts. Working closely with pastors, John developed engaging strategies that inspired congregations with a clear vision, focusing on the important message of the Great Commission. He remains dedicated to using his extensive experience to assist local ministries in their organizational development. In this critical role, he aims to encourage, equip, and empower them to fulfill their missions and broaden their influence. Additionally, he shares his insights by speaking at local churches and participating in leadership meetings, conferences, and retreats.

John earned his bachelor's degree in Communication from William Paterson University of New Jersey, graduating with high honors (Summa Cum Laude). He also received the Excellence in Interpersonal Communications Theory Award. Each year, senior faculty members select one student based on their academic accomplishments, leadership, and overall mastery of the subject area.

Besides his numerous roles in the Christian and business

sectors, John holds a special place in his heart for his beloved wife, Naomi Rivera. He also beams with pride in being the father of his two wonderful sons, Zachary and Matthew.

To learn more about Vive Consulting or to book John for an event, please send an email to:**Jrivera.vive@gmail.com**

VIVE CONSULTING

References

Chapter 1

The Holy Bible, New International Version (NIV).
Maxwell, John C. *The 21 Irrefutable Laws of Leadership: Follow Them and People Will Follow You.* Thomas Nelson, 1998.
Sinek, Simon. *Leaders Eat Last: Why Some Teams Pull Together and Others Don't.* Portfolio, 2014.

Chapter 2

The Holy Bible, New International Version (NIV).
Lewis, C.S. *Mere Christianity.* HarperOne, 2001. (Original publication: 1952).
The Collected Works of Abraham Lincoln. Edited by Roy P. Basler, Rutgers University Press, 1953. Volume 7, p. 346.
Maxwell, John C. *The 21 Irrefutable Laws of Leadership: Follow Them and People Will Follow You.* Thomas Nelson, 1998. (Quote paraphrased).
Lencioni, Patrick. *The Five Dysfunctions of a Team: A Leadership Fable.* Jossey-Bass, 2002. (Quote paraphrased).

Chapter 3

The Holy Bible, New International Version (NIV).
The Holy Bible, King James Version (KJV).
Duckworth, Angela. *Grit: The Power of Passion and Perseverance.* Scribner, 2016.
Willard, Dallas. *The Divine Conspiracy: Rediscovering Our Hidden Life in God.* HarperOne, 1998.

Chapter 4

The Holy Bible, New International Version (NIV). Proverbs 29:18. Biblica, 2011.

Maxwell, John C. *The 21 Irrefutable Laws of Leadership: Follow Them and People Will Follow You.* Thomas Nelson, 1998. (Quote paraphrased).

King, Martin Luther Jr. "I Have a Dream" speech. Delivered August 28, 1963, at the Lincoln Memorial, Washington, D.C.

King, Martin Luther Jr. *Strength to Love.* Harper & Row, 1963. (Quote paraphrased).

Keller, Helen. *The Story of My Life.* Dover Publications, 1999. (Originally published in 1903).

Blakely, Sara. *The Spanx Story: The (Mostly) Untold Story of the Entrepreneur Who Built a Billion-Dollar Business from a Pair of Pantyhose.* 2012.

Harrison, Scott. *Thirst: A Story of Redemption, Compassion, and a Mission to Bring Clean Water to the World.* Thomas Nelson, 2018.

Chapter 5

The Holy Bible: New International Version. Biblica, 2011.

Mandela, Nelson. *Conversations with Myself.* Picador, 2010.

Chapter 6

The Holy Bible, New International Version (NIV). Zondervan.

Simpson, A. K. (2011). *The Good, the Bad, and the Ugly: A Life in Politics.* HarperCollins.

Lincoln, A. (1863). *Address at the Gettysburg Cemetery.*

Buffett, W. E. (1989). *Annual Letter to Berkshire Hathaway Shareholders.*

Lutz, B. (2015). *Warren Buffett's Ground Rules: Words of Wisdom from the Partnership Letters of the World's Greatest Investor.* Wiley.

Chapter 7

Ward, William Arthur. *Thoughts of a Christian Optimist.* Droke House Publishers, 1968.

Schweitzer, Albert. *The Philosophy of Civilization.* Prometheus Books, 1987.

Graham, Billy. *Wisdom for Each Day.* Thomas Nelson, 2006.

Drucker, Peter F. *The Essential Drucker: In One Volume the Best of Sixty Years of Peter Drucker's Essential Writings on Management.* HarperBusiness, 2001.

Gandhi, Mahatma. *The Collected Works of Mahatma Gandhi*. Publications Division, Ministry of Information and Broadcasting, Government of India.

Chapter 8

Taylor, B. (2016). *Simply brilliant: How great organizations do ordinary things in extraordinary ways*. Portfolio.

Chambers, O. (1935). *My utmost for His highest*. Dodd, Mead & Company.

King, M. L. (1963). *Strength to love*. Harper & Row.

DePree, M. (1989). *Leadership is an art*. Doubleday.

Harris, A. (2010). *Do hard things: A teenage rebellion against low expectations*. Multnomah Books.

Toynbee, A. J. (1956). *A study of history (Vol. 1-12)*. Oxford University Press.

Chapter 9

Jordan, M. (1997). *Talent wins games, but teamwork and intelligence win championships*. In *The Ultimate Michael Jordan* (pp. 215–216). New York: Hachette Book Group.

Maxwell, J. C. (2001). *Teamwork makes the dream work, but a vision becomes a nightmare when the leader has a big dream and a bad team*. In *The 17 Essential Qualities of a Team Player* (p. 39). Thomas Nelson.

Teresa, M. (1985). *I can do things you cannot, you can do things I cannot; together we can do great things*. In *Mother Teresa: A Simple Path* (p. 152). New York: Ballantine Books.

Truman, H. S. (1945). *It is amazing what you can accomplish if you do not care who gets the credit*. In *Memoirs by Harry S. Truman* (Vol. 1, p. 335). Doubleday.

Blanchard, K. (1982). *None of us is as smart as all of us*. In *The One Minute Manager* (p. 77). New York: Harper & Row.

Bible Gateway. (n.d.). *Ecclesiastes 4:9-10 (NIV)*. In *The Holy Bible, New International Version*. Retrieved from https://www.biblegateway.com

Chapter 10

Roosevelt, T. (n.d.). *"If there is not the war, you don't get the general; if there is not a great occasion, you don't get a great statesman; if Lincoln had lived in a time of peace, no one would have known his name."* Retrieved from https://www.brainyquote.com

Roosevelt, T. (n.d.). *"It is hard to fail, but it is worse never to have tried to succeed."* Retrieved from https://www.brainyquote.com

Drucker, P. (2005). *The effective executive: The definitive guide to getting the right things done.* HarperBusiness.

Bonhoeffer, D. (1955). *The cost of discipleship.* Macmillan.

Swindoll, C. R. (1988). *The grace awakening.* Word Publishing.

Sinek, S. (2009). *Start with why: How great leaders inspire everyone to take action.* Penguin Group.

Bible Gateway. (n.d.). *James 1:2-4 (NIV).* In *The Holy Bible, New International Version.* Retrieved from https://www.biblegateway.com

Conclusion

Eisenhower, D. D. (1954, May 12). *Remarks at the Annual Conference of the Society for Personnel Administration.* The American Presidency Project. https://www.presidency.ucsb.edu/documents/remarks-the-annual-confer ence-the-society-for-personnel-administration

Schultz, H. (1997). *Pour Your Heart Into It: How Starbucks Built a Company One Cup at a Time.* Hyperion.

King, M. L., Jr. (1963). *Strength to Love.* Harper & Row.

Brown, B. (2012). *Daring Greatly: How the Courage to Be Vulnerable Trans-forms the Way We Live, Love, Parent, and Lead.* Gotham Books.

Keller, H. (1929). *Midstream: My later life.* Doubleday, Doran & Company.

Reflections

Augustine, S. (n.d.). *Various writings.* (Original work from the 4th-5th century).

Merton, T. (1979). *The Wisdom of the Desert.* New Directions Publishing.

Mandela, N. (1995). *Long Walk to Freedom: The Autobiography of Nelson Mandela.* Little, Brown and Company.

Testimonials About the Author

"John has been a source of incredible encouragement and wisdom in my life. His leadership, insight, and unwavering faith have profoundly impacted me and countless others. I wholeheartedly recommend him as a coach, consultant, and ministry partner."

— Rev. Dan Rainville Bethany Church, Wyckoff

"It is my privilege to endorse John Rivera as he embarks on this new chapter of ministry and leadership. I have had the blessing of witnessing John's unwavering commitment to Christ and his deep passion for advancing God's kingdom.

John exemplifies integrity in every aspect of his life and work. His leadership is marked by humility, authenticity, and a genuine desire to serve others. He has consistently demonstrated a heart for empowering leaders and encouraging them to thrive in their God-given callings.

His ability to navigate the complexities of ministry with grace and wisdom is a testament to his faith and reliance on the Lord. Whether through his writing, coaching, or ministry efforts, John has shown himself to be a vessel of encouragement and hope to all who have the privilege of working alongside him.

I am confident that his new initiatives will inspire and equip countless individuals to embrace their unique callings with resilience and purpose. I wholeheartedly support John and pray for God's continued favor and blessings over his endeavors."

— Rev. Samuel Rodriguez New Season-Lead Pastor & NHCLC President/CEO Author "Your Mess, God's Miracle!" Exec. Producer "Breakthrough" and "Flamin Hot" Movies

"I have personally known John Rivera for about 38 years. From the moment he walked into Christ Tabernacle, now known as Saints Church, he has been a man of integrity, conscientious in his walk with the Lord, and a true servant. He has always put his hand to the plow to ensure that the body of Christ and his family had everything they needed. His tenure during his decades-long work with the Billy Graham Organization has also greatly benefited the local body of Christ."

I can definitely vouch for his integrity and coaching skills, which will help other leaders become the best they can be."

— Rev. Michael Durso, Lead Pastor, Saints Church

"I am writing this endorsement and character reference for John Rivera and Vive Consulting. It has been my pleasure to know John over the years, and I can confidently say that he has been a tremendous blessing to me and Bethany Church.

As a lay leader in our church, John has consistently demonstrated his commitment, passion, and unwavering dedication to serving our congregation. His ability to utilize his gifts and business acumen has significantly enhanced our church's ministries. John has taken charge of several initiatives within the church, showcasing exceptional leadership skills and a servant's heart that has inspired many.

John has worked with our congregation and staff; he has been a blessing to everyone he has worked with. John's work has brought about positive changes and fostered a sense of community among our members and staff. He goes above and beyond to ensure that our church runs smoothly, and his contributions have had a lasting impact on our fellowship. I highly recommend and endorse John Rivera without reservation. I am confident that he will continue bringing the same excellence, integrity, and compassion to all he does."

— Rev. John James Senior Pastor, Bethany Church

"John is a highly competent individual. He is always professional and will go the extra mile to get a task done. His ego does not get in the way of the ultimate goal."

— Dr. Alfonso Wyatt Author, Public Speaker, Elder Founder, Strategic Destiny

"John Rivera is truly a servant leader. I had the pleasure of getting to know him in my former role as Media Director at Christ Church in New Jersey... John is a man of integrity and vision. I always appreciated his wise council."

— Steve Malavé University of South Florida,
Visiting Professor of Practice/Zimmerman
School Director of News & Content +
President, NAHJ - Tampa Bay

The Plan of Salvation: God's Gift for You

1. God's Love and Purpose for You

You were created by God, on purpose, and for a purpose. He loves you deeply and desires a personal relationship with you.

> *"For God so loved the world that He gave His one and only Son, that whoever believes in Him shall not perish but have eternal life."*
>
> — *John 3:16*

2. Our Problem: Sin Separates Us from God

We all have sinned—choosing our own way instead of God's way. Sin creates a gap between us and Him that we cannot bridge on our own.

> *"For all have sinned and fall short of the glory of God."*
>
> — *Romans 3:23*

> *"For the wages of sin is death, but the gift of God is
> eternal life in Christ Jesus our Lord."*

> — Romans 6:23

3. God's Solution: Jesus Christ

God sent His Son, Jesus Christ, to live a sinless life, die on the
cross for our sins, and rise again—defeating death and making a
way for us to be forgiven.

> *"But God demonstrates His own love for us in this:
> While we were still sinners, Christ died for us."*

> — Romans 5:8

> *"Jesus answered, 'I am the way and the truth and the life.
> No one comes to the Father except through Me.'"*

> — John 14:6

4. Your Response: Receive Him by Faith

Salvation is a free gift. You can't earn it—you can only receive it
by trusting Jesus as your Lord and Savior.

> *"If you declare with your mouth, 'Jesus is Lord,' and
> believe in your heart that God raised Him from the
> dead, you will be saved."*

> — Romans 10:9

5. A Simple Prayer to Begin Your New Life in Christ

If you're ready to follow Jesus, you can pray something like this from your heart:

> Lord Jesus, I believe You are the Son of God. I believe You died for my sins and rose from the dead. Today, I turn from my sins and invite You to be my Lord and Savior. Thank You for forgiving me, for giving me new life, and for making me a child of God. Amen.

6. What's Next?

If you have prayed to receive Christ, welcome to the family of God! Begin to grow in your relationship with Him by:

- Reading the Bible daily (start with the Gospel of John)
- Praying and talking to God regularly
- Connecting with a Bible-believing church
- Sharing your faith with others

> *"Therefore, if anyone is in Christ, the new creation has come: The old has gone, the new is here!"*
>
> — *2 Corinthians 5:17*

If you have made a decision to follow Jesus today, I would love to hear from you. Please share your decision with me at: Jrivera.vive@gmail.com

www.ingramcontent.com/pod-product-compliance
Lightning Source LLC
Chambersburg PA
CBHW072007040426
42447CB00009B/1523